Praise for
The Wahhabi Code

"There is no better primer for underst... ... than my friend Terence Ward's *The W......... ...s Export Extremism Globally*. Intended for young readers, it will educate their elders as well. His impeccable research destroys the prejudices and myths surrounding the distortion of Islam to benefit the Saudi royal family, western oil companies and arms dealers."

—Charles Glass, contributor *New York Review of Books*, author of *Syria Burning* and *Tribes with Flags*

"Ward's book is a compulsion of our time. I believe his experience living in Iran, Saudi Arabia, and Indonesia, and his percipient observation of day-to-day life in each Muslim country, will help us to have a more insightful view of the 'Wahhabi question.' His concern about its possible impact on the world's war and peace should be ours."

—Goenawan Mohamad, columnist, poet, founder of *Tempo* magazine, and author of *In Other Words: Forty Years of Essays from Indonesia*

"I would recommend *The Wahhabi Code* to all, especially those policy makers on issues in the Middle East and beyond."

—Cardinal Peter Kodwo Turkson, prefect of the Dicastery for Promoting Integral Human Development; former president of the Pontifical Council for Justice and Peace

"*The Wahhabi Code* reveals how a state can abet extremists and terrorists while at the same time claiming to be their enemy. Having nurtured the spread of Wahhabism and its lethal ideology throughout the world, Saudi Arabia has succeeded in silencing most media criticism. But Terence Ward's important book breaks that silence, explaining the role of Wahhabism in distorting Islam fueling the rise of ISIS and Al Qaeda. This timely book presents the truth about Wahhabism and the nature of Islam in a fresh, gripping narrative. It is a must read."

—Amed Khan, director, Global Paradigm Group, senior advisor to the ClintonGiustra Enterprise Program

"Terence Ward, an American long rooted in Italy, has written a precious book interpreting ISIS. Through massive financing of mosques and madrasas, the Wahhabis of Saudi Arabia are trying to attract traditional Islam to their radical vision, and on the other side, they have financed our politicians and the mass media to silently abide."

—**Franco Cardini, author of** *Europe and Islam, Jerusalem:*
A History, **and** *Samarkand: The Turquoise Dream*

"It is time for the United States to reconsider its 70-year relationship with the kingdom in Riyadh. Terence Ward, author of the internationally praised memoir *Searching for Hassan,* knows about Saudi Arabia: while born in Colorado, he spent his childhood in Saudi Arabia and Iran. Not only does he have a rich understanding of the deep conflicts within Islam and between nations in the Middle East, but his understanding of the subtleties of those conflicts go well beyond that of most Westerners. As tensions between Iran and Saudi Arabia have rapidly escalated, Ward reaches out with a thoughtful perspective on Saudi Arabia and the West."

—**Stanley Weiss, chairman emeritus, Business Executives for**
National Security, and columnist, *Huffington Post*

"Islam's many flavors are as misunderstood as they are mischaracterized in today's Western society. Ward's *The Wahhabi Code* demystifies one of the more virulent and violent strains of modern day Islam. Anyone interested in the relationship between religious extremism and America's ally Saudi Arabia needs to read this book."

—**Markos Kounalakis, McClatchy columnist, visiting fellow,**
Hoover Institution, and author of *Spin Wars and Spy*
Games: Global Media and Intelligence Gathering

"Fascinating, compelling and learned."

—**Joe Conason, editor-in-chief,** *The National Memo,*
author of *The Hunting of the President*

"Ward proves himself a friend of the Muslim world, whose only wish is to call attention to moderate Islam as the religion of peace it was originally intended to be."

—**Jordan Elgrably, director of** *The Markaz Review*

THE
WAHHABI
CODE

THE WAHHABI CODE

HOW THE SAUDIS SPREAD EXTREMISM GLOBALLY

TERENCE WARD

ARCADE PUBLISHING • NEW YORK

First English-language Edition 2018

Originally published in Italy under the title *Per Capire Oggi Il Medio Oriente*

Arcade Publishing books may be purchased in bulk at special discounts for sales promotion, corporate gifts, fund-raising, or educational purposes. Special editions can also be created to specifications. For details, contact the Special Sales Department, Arcade Publishing, 307 West 36th Street, 11th Floor, New York, NY 10018 or arcade@skyhorsepublishing.com.

Arcade Publishing® is a registered trademark of Skyhorse Publishing, Inc.®, a Delaware corporation.

Visit our website at www.arcadepub.com.

10 9 8 7 6 5 4 3 2 1

Library of Congress Cataloging-in-Publication Data is available on file.
Library of Congress Control Number: 2018951137

Cover design by Brian Peterson

ISBN: 978-1-951627-17-1
Ebook ISBN: 978-1-62872-972-6

Printed in the United States of America

Not Christian or Jew or Muslim not Hindu,
Buddhist, sufi, or zen. Not any religion
or cultural system. I am not from the East
or the West, not out of the ocean or up
from the ground, not natural or ethereal,
not composed of elements at all.
I do not exist, am not an entity in this world or
the next, did not descend from Adam and Eve or any
origin story. My place is placeless, a trace
of the traceless. Neither body or soul.
I belong to the beloved, have seen the two worlds
as one, and that one call to and know,
first, last, outer, inner, only that
breath breathing human being.

—Jalaladdin Rumi

The nationality of Jalaladdin Rumi—the poet and the spiritual guide known over centuries as Maulana—is still debated today. The Afghans consider him one of theirs, as he was a native of Herat in 1207, while many Iranians insist that he is the highest poet of the Sufi tradition in their Persian language. The Turks know that it was from Konya that his profoundly ecumenical and universal thinking was diffused into the world before his death in 1273.

In America, seven hundred years later, the poetry of Rumi is a bestseller.

CONTENTS

CONTENTS

THE
WAHHABI
CODE

PROLOGUE

Where am I? That is the first question.

— SAMUEL BECKETT, *THE UNNAMABLE*

This book was written to shed light on what the international media has widely chosen to ignore since September 11, 2001. In my telling in the following pages, I cite the very few brave writers and journalists who, during those years, spoke truth to power. Like Cassandra's, their lonely warnings were cries not heeded.

For decades, few newsrooms or publishers critically examined the Saudi role in the spread of extremism, and that truth remained hidden from public view. It would take the shocking death of *Washington Post* journalist Jamal Khashoggi to break the silence and finally trigger closer scrutiny.

The media today examines with a more critical eye the repression and reforms of Crown Prince Mohammad bin Salman's rule as he tries to rebrand his kingdom. Yet, now is also the time to take stock and assess the damage that Saudi Arabia has wrought on the world over the past decades. For years, global leaders at the highest levels of power have avoided speaking publicly about the roots of extremism. American administrations have even been actively complicit in its growth. And this silence has borne deadly fruit.

The journey of this book began five years ago in Florence when my young niece, Fioretta, asked me to explain the chaos in the Middle East. Bloodshed had stained the heart of Paris. One hundred thirty innocents lay dead. The bloody ISIS attacks on that November evening in 2015 left her stunned and fearful. Could it happen here in Florence? She desperately wanted answers. And so I started speaking, simply and clearly.

From our dialogue, this book was born. Published first in Italy in 2017, it is now in its fifth reprint there and has entered the curriculum of high schools in cities from north to south, from Udine to Naples.

The premise of the book is simple: a much-needed debate has long been silenced while the vastly diverse followers of mainstream Islam have been targeted and unjustly blamed for extremism. It is my deeply held conviction that when Europeans and Americans learn to pronounce the word *Wahhabi*, one and a half billion Muslims will be exonerated and freed from the cloud of guilt and discrimination cast by populist politicians who profit by spreading slander and fear.

A few years ago, Fareed Zakaria cited in a *Washington Post* op-ed a glaring fact that had gone virtually unnoticed: "According to an analysis of the Global Terrorism Database by Leif Wenar of King's College London, more than 94 percent of deaths caused by Islamic terrorism since 2001 were perpetrated by the Islamic State, al-Qaeda, and other Sunni jihadists. Iran is fighting those groups, not fueling them. *Almost every terrorist attack in the West has had some connection to Saudi Arabia* (emphasis added). Virtually none has been linked to Iran."

The "connection" that Zakaria alluded to was Wahhabism, the severe, ultra-conservative sect of Islam that is Saudi Arabia's official religion. Even now, almost twenty years after the 9/11 attacks, few know that it is also the core ideology for international terror groups such as Islamic State, Al Qaeda, the Taliban, and Boko Haram. In its extreme interpretation, the Wahhabi creed views all other Muslims as deviant heretics. Moderate Sunnis, Sufis, Shiites, Druze, Yazidis, Alawites, even whirling dervishes are branded apostates.

The Wahhabi ideology has underpinned the massacres of Sufis in Sinai, enslavement of Yazidi women in Syria, and bombings of Shiite mosques in Pakistan. Although most Muslims condemn Wahhabism as a distortion of Islam, the Saudi regime has invested tens of billions of dollars in Wahhabi charities that have exported this hardline doctrine across the Islamic World for more than forty years.

One month after the first publication of the book in Italy, the young prince Mohammad bin Salman ascended to great heights. His rise began in June 2017 when King Salman dismissed his own cousin, Nayef Al Saud, as the crown prince. Radically breaking with tradition, he appointed his son as next in line for the throne. By 2018, the new crown prince (known as MBS) had completed a masterfully orchestrated tour of America that took him from the White House to Silicon Valley, from Hollywood to Harvard, ending up on *Oprah*'s TV program.

Leading American public relations firms (The Podesta Group, Burson-Marsteller, Hill+Knowlton, King & Spalding, Brownstein Hyatt Farber Schreck, FleishmanHillard, Hogan & Hartson,

APCO, Qorvis, The Harbor Group) and a virtual army of 146 lobbyists (comprised of ex-senators, congressmen, ambassadors, and advisors) made sure that the prince enjoyed privileged red-carpet access to America's financiers in New York, San Francisco's high-tech world, and Houston's petroleum sector as well as New York's Jewish community, Los Angeles's entertainment industry, and Capitol Hill's fawning politicos.

Articles and interviews carefully promoted an air-brushed image of Saudi Arabia as a country in the midst of change. The prince was presented as a young visionary who would diversify the kingdom's economy and loosen its strict Islamic social codes, while confronting its enemies in the region, especially Iran. That vision won him fans at home and at the White House. President Trump embraced the prince as the key player in his vision for the Middle East.

MBS deftly blamed Iran for the past forty years of draconian social controls imposed by Saudi kings and Wahhabi clerics in the kingdom, saying that it was all in reaction to fears provoked by both the siege of Mecca and the Iranian Revolution in 1979. He promised that Saudi Arabia would return to "tolerant Islam." But, he made no mention of the fact that his kingdom had exported extremism across the Islamic World for decades.

According to the *Financial Times*, the kingdom's information ministry was also setting up PR "hubs" in Europe and Asia to promote the changing face of the Kingdom of Saudi Arabia to the rest of the world and to improve international perceptions.

Then, on an Istanbul morning in early October 2018, everything abruptly changed. *Washington Post* journalist Jamal Khashoggi walked into the Saudi consulate in Istanbul for paperwork related to his upcoming marriage. And he never came out. The details of what happened to him unraveled slowly.

On the morning of October 2, fifteen Saudi security and military officials had flown into Istanbul on two private jets. Among them was the kingdom's leading forensic officer carrying a bone saw. They drove to the consulate just before Khashoggi entered. Shortly after, the journalist was murdered—and was dismembered.

Commentators insisted the event could not have occurred without the approval of the Crown Prince, MBS. Global accusations were met with Saudi denials; the narrative kept changing. Videotape showed a man leaving the consulate wearing all of Khashoggi's clothes and strolling along Istanbul streets, but the imposter forgot to put on the dead man's shoes. Mr. Trump called it "the worst cover-up in history." Finally, weeks later, an admission of the rogue operation was issued by Saudi authorities with the promise of an investigation.

This dark event produced a sense of déjà-vu. Despite millions of dollars invested by Crown Prince Mohammed bin Salman in his massive PR campaign to re-brand the kingdom's image, people were reminded that Saudi Arabia has been exporting violence for years: the decapitation of the World Trade Center on 9/11; the demolition of lofty Buddhas that once towered in Bamiyan, Afghanistan; beheadings in Raqqah, Syria, by Saudi jihadis with their weaponized Wahhabi ideology imported from Riyadh, where public execution by the sword was a Friday tradition in Deera "Chop Chop" Square.

The Khashoggi case fit a pattern. Each action involved attacks outside Saudi Arabia; Saudi outrage at being accused of complicity; the blaming of rogue elements; and U.S. politicians deflecting on behalf of their "strategic ally." The common pattern typically ended with responsibility unassigned to the kingdom's rulers and their myriad ways of funding violence unquestioned.

Yet, in private. secret service agents, intelligence officers, politicos, and journalists had known these acts were part of the Saudi "double game" of publicly denying involvement in such violence while turning a blind eye to those who aid and abet it behind the scenes. Until now.

New York Times columnist Thomas Friedman's gushing praise for MBS as "the coming savior of the Arab Spring" became an embarrassment. The toxic reaction to Khashoggi's death took its toll. Fawning heads of state and corporate and finance leaders suddenly balked at attending a widely trumpeted economic summit in Riyadh called "Davos in the Desert."

The recklessness of MBS unnerved even staunch political supporters. A troubling pattern could easily be seen. The Saudi bombing campaign launched by the Crown Prince across Yemen in 2015 had reduced the neighboring country to what the UN described as "the world's worst humanitarian disaster." Millions suffered, on the verge of starvation. There was also the radical blockade of neighboring Qatar, with the threat of an invasion; the bizarre detention of princes and businessmen in the Riyadh

Ritz-Carlton; the strange kidnapping of the Lebanese prime minister; the rupture with Canada over a foreign minister's tweet about a jailed activist.

The Khashoggi Affair pulled all those events back into the public eye; and thrust the kingdom in the most uncomfortable light since the 9/11 attacks in 2001.

The American edition of *The Wahhabi Code: How the Saudis Spread Extremism Globally* was released just as Turkish police searched the parks of Istanbul for Khashoggi's body parts.

That week, on a humid day in Singapore, I was taken completely by surprise when a producer of Christiane Amanpour's called me from London. She insisted that a live interview in their CNN studios would be best, not a video link from Southeast Asia. By mid-December, I walked into their offices on Great Marlborough Street and Christiane greeted me warmly. We had first met in New York years before. She had not lost an ounce of her journalistic courage. As we chatted, she confessed that for months, she had been searching for someone willing to talk about the legacy of Wahhabism.

Fifteen minutes later, she began our interview. "So your book, the premise of it is that an overlooked aspect of the global terrorism that we face today is how much of it is inspired by Wahhabism, Salafism, that is emblematic of Saudi Arabia. Tell me about that."

We discussed many issues, and as our time drew to a close, I said: "Let's be sane about our next steps because we can't afford other crises [like ISIS] because a strategic relationship—that doesn't share democracy, freedom of worship, freedom of speech, freedom of the press or human rights—is only transactional [based on oil]."

Christiane concluded: "The most interesting thing about this moment, I guess, is that all these things were off the table. They could never be discussed during bilateral relations. Now that's changed—should Saudi's main allies decide to go that route—because in the aftermath of Khashoggi, that's all changed."

In fact, a new counter-narrative had begun. For the first time, Washington politicians united to call for an end of American military support of the Saudi war in Yemen and the need to re-examine America's "strategic partnership."

In that same month of December, two months after the grisly murder, the entire US Senate voted unanimously to condemn the Crown Prince for his responsibility in Khashoggi's death. It was a rare moment of unity for the unruly Congress. Once-loyal Republican Senator Lindsey Graham called MBS a "wrecking ball" and raged "there's no smoking gun, there's a smoking saw," while Senator Rand Paul spoke of "ending weapons sales to Saudi Arabia" as punishment.

The visionary young reformer's sheen was tarnished. Many wondered whether MBS was a rising dictator whose inexperience and rash decisions were destabilizing the world's most volatile region. A forensic look at Riyadh's wider impact on recent events is also troubling. Geopolitically, the Saudi talent at lighting fires beyond their borders has spawned other tragedies that will haunt our children.

One can even argue that that the looming breakup of Europe— as the continent lurches to the right into fascist authoritarianism—

began with the dawn of Islamic State. The attacks in Paris, London, Brussels, Nice, and Berlin, the biblical flood of refugees fleeing Syria into Europe—all stoked fears of immigration, fed Islamophobia, and fueled populist sentiment. The Brexit vote, the victories of nationalists such as Viktor Orban in Hungary, Boris Johnson in the UK, and Matteo Salvini in Italy—are repercussions of recklessness in Riyadh.

Only time will tell how this new chapter of the House of Saud under MBS's rule will unfold. Can the world's most conservative society truly make groundbreaking reforms? Or will changes be superficial, designed to please the West? One may celebrate the lifting of the ban on women driving or the opening three hundred cinemas by 2030 as a dramatic break with the past. But one may also ask about the imprisoned and tortured female activists who led the "right to drive" campaign. Or those women who say "We are our own guardians," rebuking MBS's refusal to end the "guardianship law" that places every woman in Saudi Arabia under the control of a male guardian. Or the three thousand prisoners of conscience documented by Amnesty International. Or the countless suffering innocents in neighboring Yemen.

A blowback is building. In his May 4, 2020, article for Bloomberg "How MBS Hit a Dead End in Washington," Bobby Ghosh described the current mood:

> *MBS has few friends in Washington—and the army of lobbyists he maintains there is of limited use in a crisis. Instead, the prince is as close to a pariah as a senior member of the royal family has*

ever been in the seventy-five years of the Saudi-American alli-
ance. He is under near-constant attack from all quarters in
Washington over a wide range of issues.

Fareed Zakaria, in his April 21, 2016, *Washington Post* piece, "Saudi
Arabia, the Devil We Know," had described the impact of Wahhabism in the Islamic world and in particular his ancestral Pakistan:

> *I believe that Saudi Arabia bears significant responsibility for the*
> *spread of a cruel, intolerant, and extremist interpretation of*
> *Islam—one that can feed directly into jihadi thinking. This glo-*
> *balized Wahhabism has destroyed much of the diversity within*
> *Islam, snuffing out the liberal and pluralistic interpretations of*
> *the religion in favor of and arid, intolerant one.*
>
> *Saudi funding of Islamic extremism has not ended, and its per-*
> *nicious effects can be seen from Pakistan to Indonesia. Saudi*
> *Arabia has created a monster in the world of Islam that threatens*
> *Saudi Arabia and the West. The Saudi monarchy must reform*
> *itself and its export of ideology.*

Most Muslims wholeheartedly agree with Mr. Zakaria. Substantial
reforms must be made by Islamic scholars to those Wahhabi texts
that have inspired so many jihadi groups. MBS has assured the
world that such reforms will be forthcoming.

If scholars carefully edit and reform the texts, which are
attributed to the founder of the doctrine, Muhammad Abdul Wahhab, perhaps change can take place.

New editions of religious books can be printed; students can be taught differently; and imams can be persuaded to adapt more open tolerant views. But unless this is done with a firm commitment by leading clerics and the royal family publicly voicing a clear new vision that accepts *all* other Muslims—Shias, Sufis, and Sunnis—and non-Muslims as God's children. Otherwise, the threat of re-emerging violence will be always simmering.

A Saudi scholar at Georgetown, Abdullah Alaoudh, openly challenged the "tolerant Islam" campaign of the Crown Prince in his compelling interview on Al-Jazeera on June 28, 2019: "The 'moderate Islam' campaign by MBS is a fake campaign against extremism. He has been targeting the moderate voices and selling this to the West as curtailing religious establishment, while, in fact, he's curtailing moderate voices calling for democratic demands at the same time empowering these extremists like al-Fawzan who in return legitimize his own rule."

This is troubling news. This hardline cleric, Sheikh al-Fawzan, sits as a member of the state-sponsored Council of Senior Scholars. From the outset, MBS had embraced him as a father figure. In 2017, Mr. al-Fawzan declared that the Shia and other Muslims who did not follow Wahhabi beliefs were infidels and that anyone who disagreed with his interpretation was an infidel. In effect, he excommunicated all Saudi Shias, a sizeable minority whose ancestral lands lie amid the Gulf oil fields.

In April 2019, thirty-three Shia were beheaded for treason. Many wondered why the Saudi King offered critics another human rights issue after the brutal death of Kahshoggi. But these executions served a clear purpose: to strike fear in the Saudi Shia population while rallying the royal family's ultra-conservative Wahhabi base. In the end, to be Shia in Saudi Arabia has always been a complicated affair.

Violence against Shia communities is deeply rooted in the Saudi Kingdom's DNA. Like African Americans in the Deep South, the Shia have suffered discrimination and suspicion from the Wahhabi ruling elite since the founding of the country in 1932. Those who were executed in April included protestors who were arrested and convicted of terror-related crimes during the Arab Spring demonstrations five years before in 2011 –12. Some were underage at the time of their arrest. Amnesty International protested in vain that the legal proceedings "violated international fair trial standards which relied on confessions extracted through torture."

Mr. al-Fawzan also issued a fatwa in September 2018 declaring that any political dissidents who disagreed with the kingdom's rulers stood guilty of treason and should be executed. A month later, Jamal Khashoggi was assassinated. Mr. Al-Fawzan had given MBS the green light.

"MBS is always obsessed with attacking those who have more popularity." Abdullah Alaoudh explained further in his Al Jazeera interview: "My father Salman Al Awdah had 14 million Twitter followers, double of the King, and he promoted the democratic discourse. In 2011, he circulated a petition to transform the state into a constitutional monarchy where: minorities are protected; women are empowered; people are represented in an elected parliament; and rights are guaranteed." His discourse was acceptable to the Saudi public and his popularity grew. Then 2017, when the

Qatar controversy broke, he tweeted a prayer asking for reconciliation. MBS did not take it lightly; two hours after his tweet, state security arrived at his house to arrest him.

In the sprawling al-Ha'yr prison, south of Riyadh, the dissident sheikh has been sentenced to death for treason as an "enemy of the state." He has been joined by other prisoners of conscience, prominent women's rights campaigners. Loujain al-Hathloul has been held since 2018 for her campaign against the driving ban and the oppressive women guardianship system. Evidently, MBS did not want give any credit to women activists. He understood that the women's movement in Saudi Arabia is not simply about driving. It's about rights.

In that same prison languished another famed reformist, Abdullah Al-Hamid. who had called for constitutional reforms as far back as 1990. This poet, scholar, and political prisoner—called "the Mandela of Saudi Arabia" by Jamal Khashoggi—died in custody on April 24, 2020, after being denied a medical care for his weak heart.

Crown Prince Mohommad bin Salman, now embodies a strange distinction: shaping most repressive regime in recent Saudi history—and also, in some respects, the most reformist.

Important questions linger. How secure is the future of Prince Salman? Has his popularity suffered from the austerity program and his crackdown on dissidents? Will he be pushed aside by his own royal family who feel he has gone too far? Are there conspiracies being hatched as I write?

Ben Hubbard, the *New York Times* Middle East correspondent, confirmed in his book *MBS, the Rise of Mohammad bin Salman* that "the Crown Prince feared plots by a range of rivals." This concern gave birth to his repressive hacking cyberwarfare campaign using shadowy spyware contractors. Dissenting voices on social media have been targeted. Pervasive fear has all but silenced Saudi society. And the hacking campaign even reached the cell phones of Amazon CEO Jeff Bezos and Mr. Hubbard.

"In today's Saudi Arabia, no one is safe from the state repression apparatus, even royal family members who fall out of line," said Adam Coogle, deputy director of Human Rights Watch. The hopes of a more democratic system based on institutions and rights have evaporated. Many suggest that the new Saudi Arabia has at its heart a draconian police state obsessed with snuffing out any dissent.

Meanwhile, MBS's bold "Vision 2030" to diversify the Saudi economy remains in doubt. The recent Corona-virus crisis and steep drop in oil revenues has led to an unprecedented austerity budget. This downturn has put the brakes on his eye-catching megaprojects, including the futuristic city of Neom on the Red Sea and a 334-square-kilometer entertainment, arts, and nature site on the outskirts of the capital, Riyadh. Without a healthy budget, foreign investment, and foreign skilled labor, his dream appears like a mirage.

When Florence shut its doors during the Covid-19 lockdown, we had just returned from a tour to two literary festivals that ended in

India with the Jaipur Literature Festival. Two months before had been in Bali at the Ubud Writers & Readers Festival. Apart from speaking there, I had been invited by the festival's satellite program to present the book in Jakarta at Paramadina University and the Universitas Islam Negara (UIN). With each audience, I spoke about the need to protect Indonesia's traditional Islam from the puritanical, rigid Wahhabi import. In Java's religious schools, decades of funding by Saudi Arabia's World Muslim League had sowed the seeds of radicalism. Current estimates suggested that 25 percent of Indonesian Muslims followed the Wahhabi (Salafi) path.

At both universities, I was surprised that the message was received so enthusiastically by hundreds of students, an overwhelming majority of young women. Both presidents told me they were in full agreement. Dr. Pipip, President of Paramadina, thanked me warmly and confessed that the issue had been under the radar for years. The UIN president told me that now this debate had been openly voiced in their auditorium, they could talk about it openly. The great fear of self-censorship had been lifted.

That following afternoon, Indonesia's finance minister, Dr. Sri Mulyani Indrawati, invited me to speak to her senior aides at the ministry. Already, Jakarta newspapers had published her bold declaration to deradicalize her ministry. This progressive, charismatic woman had garnered international praise as managing director of the World Bank and, in 2018, been given the prestigious Best Minister award at the World Government Summit.

She had summoned me there for a reason. I was being used to frame a message to her staff. Minister Indrawati began our meeting by pointing out, "The founding principles of Indonesia are based on *Pancasila*—'unity in diversity' and the respect of all our faiths. We cannot lose sight of this."

"And, sadly," I added, "there are radicals, who are not nationalists, that dream of imposing an Islamic State."

Minister Indrawati raised her voice again. "The nation's principles must be respected, and those in government who do not agree, must leave their positions."

I then raised a delicate point to her aides.

"Did you know that Saudi clerics are considering destroying the steps to the holy cave of Hira where the prophet received his first revelation, and even the entire cave itself? Some even talk of destroying the Prophet's tomb in Medina?"

They all looked surprised. The Cave of Hira is one of the favored sites for all Indonesians on pilgrimage. It takes two hours to climb up the Mountain of Illumination, called Jabal al Nour, overlooking Mecca. There, they relive the moment on that fateful night in 610 when Mohammad was commanded by angel Gabriel to recite. It is there that the first words of divine revelation descended upon the Prophet to light up the universe.

"Hardline Wahhabis," I explained, "judge Indonesians who visit both sites as polytheists. They believe that prayers can only go to God—not to any human. Not even the prophet can be revered through prayer. Only God. And those who pray to saints or the prophet they view as impure, as apostates."

I could feel their unease hearing this.

"We all know that Indonesian Islam," I continued, "was brought to Java by the *Wali Songo*, the Nine Saints, first by Malik Ibrahim from Persia and Samarkand and then the others. People still flock to their shrines today as pilgrims to pray. It was a gentler Sufi Islam that spread so quickly in Java, not the harsh, fundamentalist Wahhabism of the desert. Your traditional Islam embraces tolerance of all faiths. This is Indonesia's identity—the question is how to protect it from the radicals."

Minister Indrawati then spoke.

"Before the presidential election," she told us all, "this was not a major priority for the government."

A hush fell in the conference room.

"Now it is!" she concluded emphatically.

All her aides understood.

Halfway across the world, a larger issue looms in the Middle East. A shared loathing and fear of Iran has led to a rapprochement between Saudi Arabia and Israel. Bound together as allies, they have embodied the Middle Eastern maxim, "The enemy of my enemy is my friend." MBS now speaks of "Saudi First," dismissing the age-old Palestinian question that shaped Arab politics toward Israel for generations.

When President Trump tore up America's nuclear deal with Iran in 2017, America enacted a "maximum pressure" campaign with Tehran, imposing crippling sanctions and travel bans, accompanied by saber rattling. Since then, the Crown Prince and Prime Minister Netanyahu have aggressively lobbied the president to launch a preemptive bombing campaign. They argue there is nothing to stop Iran's race for the bomb. America may soon be dragged into a new Middle East war, triggered by these two allies. We should be very wary.

Trump, Netanyahu, and King Salman stand alone. Aggression against Iran risks rupturing ties with Europe and NATO, while provoking conflict with both Russia and China. If missiles are launched and bombs fall like they did in the Aramco oilfields last year, the narrow Strait of Hormuz—the gateway in and out of the Persian Gulf—will surely be closed to oil tankers until the shooting ends.

Oil prices will spike astronomically. Markets will crumble. Shortages will occur. Lights of the industrial world will dim. It will be a time for lighting candles, unless cooler heads prevail. Perhaps this is the moment to review America's "strategic partnership" and not be lured in yet again to another conflagration without end.

Saudi-American relations were never based on shared values of democracy, equality, freedom of speech, or the freedom of worship. In the 1945 Quincy Agreement between President Franklin D. Roosevelt and King Abdul Aziz, only the free flow of oil" was ensured, along with the US pledge to protect the Saud family. But even realpolitik has its limits.

Another brave Saudi scholar, Madawi al-Rasheed, recently offered her sobering views in a recent talk entitled "The Saudi Lie." The noted professor at the Middle East Center of the London School of Economics spoke at Griffith University, Australia, in October 26, 2019:

MBS declared Saudi Arabia a bastion of "tolerant Islam," but of course, the country is long associated with exporting radical Islamic interpretations that created the Global Jihadi movement in the 1980s during the Afghan war. This brand of Islam is known as Wahhabiya, *the state religion. And for decades, for 250 years, it has been the dominant religious interpretation that successive Saudi regimes adopted. MBS presents himself as a partner in terrorism, but we all know that the religious roots of that terrorism that sprang in the 1980's originated nowhere but in Saudi Arabia.*

In her ground-breaking book *Black Wave*, Lebanese journalist Kim Ghattas charts the forty-year rivalry between Saudi Arabia and Iran that unraveled culture, religion, and collective memory across the region. She begins by raising the heart-wrenching question lingering on everyone's lips in the Middle East, "What happened to us?" Ghattas describes how "The question haunts us in the Arab and Muslim world. We repeat it like a mantra. You will hear it from Iran to Syria, from Saudi Arabia to Pakistan, and in my own country, Lebanon. For us, the past is a different country one that is not mired in the horrors of sectarian killings; a more vibrant place, without the crushing intolerance of religious zealots and, seemingly endless, amorphous wars."

In her narrative, she explains how reactionary forces spread chaos across the region for forty years beginning with the pivotal date of 1979. "The weaponisation of sectarianism, women's rights, the frustrated hopes of the Arab spring, the rise of Al-Qaeda and Islamic State cast darkness across the Middle East for decades. . . . Obfuscation and the feigning of ignorance would become favourite forms of Saudi subterfuge to evade responsibility for any violence or intolerance connected to the kingdom." That is, until Khashoggi's savage murder.

The curtain has fallen on King Salman's rule. Whatever direction MBS takes his country into the future, there remains an unpaid debt that the Saudi Kingdom owes the Islamic World, an atonement. Last year, I was invited by James Cuno, the President of the J. Paul Getty Trust, to speak at the noted museum in Los Angeles on the topic: "From the Buddhas of Bamiyan to the Temples of Palmyra: Why Is the World's Cultural Heritage Being Erased?" In this time of reckoning, when America, the UK, Belgium, and France are confronting crimes of history from their imperial past, Saudi Arabia should not escape the same scrutiny. The time has come to examine this past in the cold light of day.

May this account written for a sixteen-year-old Florentine cast light on that darkness.

To begin unravelling our delicate story, we now must travel to Paris and that bleak day that dawned in November 2015.

ON PARISIAN BOULEVARDS

Behold! The caravan of civilization has been ambushed.
Everywhere fools are in charge.

—Jalaladdin Rumi

WINTER 2015

Pale morning light. Early Saturday. November 14. I stare out my window, stunned as a storm sweeps in from the east. News comes in from Paris. Dead *citoyens* lie scattered across the city. On Boulevard Voltaire, in Le Carillon bar and La Belle Equipe restaurant, outside À la Bonne Bière café, inside the Bataclan theater. Here, in Florence, the Arno churns with rainfall from the night before. Tears for the fallen.

"What now?" I ask myself. Yet, I know the answer. It is ISIS, the Islamic State of Iraq and Syria. And the hunt for those responsible will lead police and journalists to Brussels, Europe's epicenter of Wahhabism, where it has been incubating for decades.

I search the internet. I Google the word *Wahhabi*. Only four articles appear, all from 2014. One is posted on an Indian website, the other by British journalist Patrick Cockburn in *The*

Independent, another by David Kirkpatrick in the *New York Times,* and the last in *The Economist.* Nothing else.

By noon, the body count grows—130 dead and 368 injured.

ISIS has claimed responsibility for the murders. But who are these people? And who has inspired and funded ISIS?

For the average citizen, this answer seems lost in the mists of time, in the distant fog of Middle Eastern wars that began with the American invasion of Iraq and later spread across Syria. This region of the world, now cursed with anarchy, leaves most questions unanswered.

Searching for clues, I open Kirkpatrick's *New York Times* article, "ISIS' Harsh Brand of Islam Is Rooted in Austere Saudi Creed," in which he writes:

> *For their guiding principles, the leaders of the Islamic State . . . are open and clear about their almost exclusive commitment to the Wahhabi movement. . . . The group circulates images of Wahhabi religious textbooks from Saudi Arabia in the schools it controls. Videos from the group's territory have shown Wahhabi texts plastered on the sides of an official missionary van. Bernard Haykel of Princeton has described al-Baghdadi's creed as "a kind of untamed Wahhabism."*

Other clues lay inside the *Economist* article, "The Other Beheaders:"

> *There is not much difference between a death sentence in the jihadists' "Islamic State" and in Saudi Arabia, a country seen as*

a crucial Western ally in the fight against ISIS. Nor, indeed, is there much difference between the two entities in other applications of a particularly merciless brand of sharia, or Islamic law, including public whippings and the right for victims of crime to claim eye-for-an-eye revenge. Dissidents in Raqqa, the Syrian town that is ISIS's proto-capital, say all 12 of the judges who now run its court system, adjudicating everything from property disputes to capital crimes, are Saudis. The group has also created a Saudi-style religious police, charged with rooting out vice and shooing the faithful to prayers. And as in ISIS-ruled zones, where churches and non-Sunni mosques have been blown up or converted to other uses.

I begin writing an article full of fury and anguish, but not with the venom of Oriana Fallaci or her uncontrollable hate. I write with deep affection for these ancient lands where I lived for over thirty years. I write with urgency to speak on behalf of these people, family and friends that I have known and loved my entire life. And I write for a troubled world under threat.

After finishing the piece, I sent it to my friend Stanley Weiss, chairman emeritus of Business Executives for National Security and expert on international politics. Stanley's reaction was unusual—he was upset.

"Why haven't I heard anything about this?" he asked over the telephone. A sophisticated, cosmopolitan gentleman with long security experience and a global awareness of looming dangers, Stanley does not enjoy being taken by surprise. He ended with, "This may be the most important article that I've read this year."

A month later in December on the BBC, five experts are posed the question "Is Saudi Arabia to Blame for the Islamic State?" Saudi-born Madawi al-Rashid, visiting professor at the Middle East Centre at the London School of Economics, answered with yet more clues:

The Wahhabis were given full control of the religious, social and cultural life of the kingdom. As long as the Wahhabi preachers preached that Saudis should obey their rulers, the al-Saud family was happy. In the 1960s and 1970s the Arab world was full of revolutionary ideas. The Saudi government thought the Wahhabis were a good antidote, because they provide an alternative narrative about how to obey rulers and not interfere in politics. In the 1980s, King Fahd established a printing press to publish Korans, sent for free to different parts of the world. They established Al-Madinah University to teach religion to students from around the world.

When Afghanistan was invaded by the Soviet Union, Wahhabism was instrumentalized by the Saudi regime. It inspired young Muslim men to go to Afghanistan to fight a jihad against the Russian infidels. Wahhabism benefitted from the arrival of the Muslim Brotherhood, who were exiled from places like Egypt, Syria and Iraq in the 1950s and 1960s. Saudi Arabia welcomed them. A lot of them became religious teachers so the fusion between this Wahhabi tradition, and the organizational skills of other Islamists, led to the emergence of a new trend in Saudi Arabia; the Islamist trend, what is referred to as the Islamic awakening.

Soon after, my article was published in the *Huffington Post* on January 14, 2016. Stanley's comment introduced the piece.

FIVE SAUDI IMPERIAL PROJECTS THE WEST HAS SLEPT THROUGH
By Stanley A. Weiss and Terence Ward

Horrified by the news that Saudi Arabia would set a record for beheadings in 2015 while continuing to fund radical Islamic groups across the world, I wrote a column last October arguing that it was time for the United States to reconsider its seventy-year relationship with the kingdom in Riyadh. After the piece was posted, one of the friends I heard from was Terence Ward, author of the internationally praised memoir, *Searching for Hassan*. Ward knows about Saudi Arabia: while born in Colorado, he spent his childhood in Saudi Arabia and Iran. Not only does he have a rich understanding of the deep conflicts within Islam and between nations in the Middle East, but as a man who speaks six languages— including Arabic and Farsi—his understanding of the subtleties of those conflicts go well beyond that of most Westerners. As tensions between Iran and Saudi Arabia have rapidly escalated this month over Riyadh's execution of a high-profile Shiite cleric, Ward reached out with a thoughtful perspective on Saudi Arabia and the West. I print it in full. . . .

Since 2001, Western leaders have discretely avoided the naked truth—today's Islamic terrorism is deeply rooted in the Saudi

Wahhabi faith. First with al-Qaeda's 9/11 attacks and now with ISIS bombings in Brussels and slaughter in Paris, the West's rush for revenge ignores those roots yet again.

Both al-Qaeda and ISIS needed failed states to create their base: in Afghanistan, and in northern Iraq and eastern Syria, respectively. But to flourish, they needed funding and ideology, which were imported from Saudi Arabia.

To be blunt, where is decapitation a public sport? Only in Riyadh and Raqqa. Growing up in Saudi Arabia, I witnessed crowds gather on Friday in "chop-chop square" to watch the medieval spectacle. The recent forty-seven beheadings remind us again of this uniquely Saudi custom. Now, it has now been exported to Syria where YouTube clips spread the spectacle to the world. But they share more than executions. Few know that as Syrian and Iraqi towns fell to ISIS, Saudi textbooks replaced what was in classrooms before. So, if any Western leaders seriously want to end the radicalization of young Muslims, they must look no further than the father of the radical faith followed by both terror groups—found in the Saudi religious industrial complex. Wahhabism. In Saudi Arabia, there are no churches, synagogues, or Hindu temples. Wahhabism is not a religion of tolerance. The chilling fact is that in three decades, the Saudis have launched five imperial projects in support of Wahhabism—all sources of today's jihadists.

The first project in Pakistan began when General Zia ul-Haq, after seizing power in 1977, imposed sharia law and then gave carte blanche to create countless Saudi-funded Wahhabi madrasas—Islamic schools—across the country to indoctrinate young children and fill the gap of a collapsed education system. Targeting refugee camps full of vulnerable Afghans fleeing the Soviet invasion, the Wahhabi movement found its base.

The second project in Afghanistan was born in these refugee camps when a new generation came of age, calling themselves "the students" or "Taliban." In 1994, Mullah Omar and fifty madrasa students launched out from Quetta as a fighting force crossing the border, seizing Kandahar, and then taking Kabul in 1996. By 1997, Saudi employees were traveling for free as tourists on government-paid holidays to visit the Islamic Emirate of Afghanistan with their families so they could witness the "true Islam." Mullah Omar was invited on Hajj by the Saudi monarch in 1998. He then ordered the Bamiyan Buddhas blown apart in March 2001, in keeping with the iconoclast Saudi vision. The free tourist trips from Riyadh ended abruptly on September 11 that same year.

The third project was al-Qaeda's global jihad financed by Wahhabi funders that began with financing foreign fighters in Soviet-occupied Afghanistan and climaxed with the Twin Towers attack. It's enough to remember that fifteen of the nineteen hijackers, as well as al-Qaeda's founder Osama bin Laden, hailed from Saudi Arabia.

The fourth imperial project is named ISIS, also known as ISIL (Islamic State of Iraq and the Levant), or DAESH (an acronym formed from the Arabic transliteration of ISIS). Its mother was America's Iraq invasion. Its father was Saudi Arabia's eager Wahhabi funders and a defiant ideology that capitalized on the Sunni humiliation in Iraq and Syria. Now, the Sunni–Shia conflagration is tearing apart both countries and the region is ablaze with four civil wars. Of course, Saudis argue this was all started to combat

Iran's imperial ambitions, but the truth is that Sunnis, not the Shia, have mastered their macabre monopoly on suicide bombings. This is the terror that was exported to Paris.

The fifth imperial project lies in Western Europe—in all madrasas funded by Saudi money and staffed with Wahhabi-trained imams from Paris to Brussels, Antwerp and Rotterdam, from Marseilles to Birmingham. Thousands of mosques and schools have trained a new generation of Muslims in the rigid and intolerant faith imported from Riyadh, without any local government supervision. And now these seeds planted by Saudi Arabia are bearing fruit under a newly re-named *Salafist* banner. This *Salafi* term has been cleverly promoted to disguise any connection to Wahhabism or the Saudi origins, and it has worked. International journalists now solely use the word *Salafi* as if describing a widespread conservative current in Islam today.

Over forty years ago, Belgium's King Baudouin cut a deal with Saudi Arabia's King Faisal. In exchange for cheap oil, Baudouin gave the Saudis a ninety-nine-year lease on the former Oriental Pavilion for the Grande Mosque. At the same time, the Belgians allowed Saudi trained imams to preach to the growing numbers of Maghrebi immigrants coming into the country. This gave the House of Saud carte blanche for three generations to spread their doctrine of Wahhabism in rigid religious schools, setting up tension between the more moderate Tunisian and Moroccan traditions and the Saudi-financed teachings. Today, there are seventy-seven mosques in Brussels, which is not only the capital of the Europe Union and NATO, it is also the capital of European Wahhabism and Islamic terrorism.

From the 2001 assassination of Ahmad Shah Massoud—the famed Afghan anti-Taliban leader—to the 2004 Madrid train bombings, from the Paris shootings at the Charlie Hebdo offices, to last year's killings at the Jewish museum in Brussels and this summer's foiled shooting spree on a high-speed train, from the Paris massacres and the recent bombings in Brussels, all investigators' lines of inquiry have led to Europe's "ground zero" of terrorism—the Brussels suburb of Molenbeek. This should not be surprising. Only last year, Belgium was riveted by the trial of forty-six people who were found guilty of belonging to *Sharia4Belgium*, a group that recruited volunteers to fight in Syria with ISIS. And Belgium has the other dubious honor of sending ISIS more foreign fighters per capita than any other country in Europe.

The element that all five imperial projects share is the Wahhabi doctrine—extremist, fundamentalist, and exclusionist. This creed is surprisingly new to Islam. Only two hundred years old, it carries the name of its firebrand founder, Muhammad Abdul Wahhab. The Christian equivalent would be a union of two groups: the Jehovah Witness and the American racist Christian group, the Ku Klux Klan. The Wahhabi doctrine views all other Muslims as deviant, decadent, and dangerous heretics, deserving no mercy. Moderate Sunnis, Sufis, Shia, Ismailis, Druze, Yazidis, Alawites, even the whirling dervishes are *all* enemies—impure, fallen Muslims. Apostates all. Of course, non-Muslims fall under the same umbrella of loathing. No common humanity exists. There is no possible dialogue. Their sharia is the only covenant. All non-Wahhabi believers are expendable. It is high time to point out publically the differences existing between the many variants of traditional Islam and the virulent hostility with which the newly created Wahhabi sect views everyone else, be they Muslims or not.

Make no mistake; the Saudi Wahhabis are on a global mission of conversion. Their dream is to change forever a faith that once was tolerant, back when Christians, Jews, and Muslims lived side by side in the cosmopolitan Levant's multi-cultural mélange of dialects and faiths along the Eastern Mediterranean—from Alexandria to Beirut, from Damascus to Istanbul.

In the non-Arabic world of Southeast Asia—in Indonesia with over 190 million Muslim faithful—the mood is still reminiscent of those more tolerant times. Islam arrived there with Persian and Gujarati merchants who sailed into tropical ports with their mystical and very tolerant Islam. Their faith was grounded in open-minded Sufi beliefs and traditions. This is why Islam spread so quickly across the archipelago. Had these early merchants offered instead, a rigidly austere Wahhabi "desert-bound message," there would have been few takers.

Now, it is only in Indonesia that a forceful repudiation of the Islamic State has surfaced. It has come from the powerful Nahdlatul Ulama party, called NU, that counts as members over fifty million Muslims. Their recent film of ISIS beheadings features the voice-over of their revered leader and former Indonesian president, Abdurrahman Wahid, singing a Javanese mystical poem: *"Many who memorize the Quran and Hadith love to condemn others as infidels while ignoring their own infidelity to God, their hearts and minds still mired in filth."*

This campaign for a liberal, pluralistic Islam comes from a country with a rich Hindu and Buddhist past, where Sunnis and Shias live together in harmony. This tradition of Islam stresses nonviolence, inclusiveness, and acceptance of other religions. It was borne from the Sufi tradition. All commentators and pundits who have been asking for a "reformation in Islam," needn't look further. The Islam that they are searching for exists in Indonesia. And it is the antidote to jihadism.

It is this faith that historically spread across the islands of Indonesia, Malaysia, and Bengal. And it is this faith that was also rooted in the beating heart of the Islamic world: Mecca. Few Westerners know that for one thousand years the holy city of Mecca was the center of the Sufi universe, where music, dance, and ecstatic prayer celebrated the divine and faithful gathered at shrines and graves of saints.

When the Wahhabi-backed House of Saud conquered the Hejaz, Mecca, and Medina in 1924, the state of Saudi Arabia was declared, and Wahhabism was proclaimed the official religion. In less than one hundred years, the Saud family and their Wahhabi benefactors erased the city's rich, mystic past, including historical sites like the Prophet's house in Mecca, along with that of his daughter Fatimeh. Homes of the Prophet's wives are now parking lots. All those pilgrims who embark on their Hajj arrive in Mecca only to find a city that has been cleansed of its diverse layers of Islamic history.

Alas, virtually every aspect and corner Islam today has now been penetrated by Wahhabi influence, thanks to 200 billion dollars spent over the last thirty years in a strategic campaign to promote Wahhabism around the world. Thousands of Saudi-funded madrasas have indoctrinated countless young minds with the Wahhabi doctrine in Belgium, France, Holland, Germany, Bosnia, Kosovo, and the UK, as well as across the Arab world. At the moment, the economies of the Middle East and North Africa are not creating job opportunities for the tens of millions of young students of both sexes who are the ones most vulnerable and easily enticed to join ISIS.

Additionally, Saudi money has strategically silenced virtually all criticism in the international media. Saudi ownership of the largest Arab media outlets (newspapers, magazines, and TV channels) has been crucial in keeping their imperial projects from being discussed openly in the Arab world. Meanwhile, strategic payments of Saudi and Qatari money have bought the deafening silence of western media and politicians. Robust sales of military weaponry and prime real estate in major capitals, such as Rome, Paris, and London, have quieted any visible criticism from senior political figures. Quite simply, articles that may expose the depth of influence are simply not published.

With each passing day, the royal House of Saud plays a dangerous double game—posing as allies of the West, while allowing funding to pour into terrorist networks. This way they quiet criticism from their zealous Wahhabi clerics at home. In Palermo, Sicilians pay for "protection" the same way. Ironically, over a decade ago on July 13, 2005, Stuart Levey, US Treasury Under Secretary for Terrorism and Financial Intelligence, pointed out in Congressional testimony that "wealthy Saudi financiers and charities have funded terrorist organizations and causes that support terrorism and the ideology that fuels the terrorists' agenda. Even today, we believe that Saudi donors may still be a significant source of terrorist financing, including for the insurgency in Iraq. Saudi Arabia-based and funded organizations remain a key source for the promotion of ideologies used by terrorists and violent extremists around the world."

Today, little has changed.

The conclusions are chilling. Until the Saudi religious roots in today's crisis are unearthed and examined in the cold light of day, history will only repeat itself from Raqaa to Paris, from Riyadh to Brussels, from Nice to San Bernardino. As George Soros reminds us, we also live in an "Age of Fallibility." Our assumptions of reality must be re-assessed each day. Turning a blind eye to Saudi Arabia's imperial ambitions since 9/11, has led us to this moment of reflection. More importantly, Western leaders should take note of the courageous Indonesians who so openly and profoundly denounce ISIS and Wahhabism. There is indeed a grand difference between Muslims, and this must be amplified in the ongoing debate today.

Unless the Saudis show tolerance and allow churches, temples, and synagogues to be built in Arabia (which is highly unlikely), the EU and the US should take a firm position and legally cease all Saudi funding—public and private—destined for mosques and Islamic schools in their respective countries. Leaders need to openly speak about Wahhabism (just as they did with Baathism) and end the deafening silence purchased by petro-dollars. From Capitol Hill to the EU corridors in Brussels, an oft-whispered claim insists that the royal family is the lesser of two evils. This smacks of irony. The House of Saud has *always* been Wahhabi.

Now, the West must wake to the coming storm. And, we all must pray that no conspiracy is afoot within Pakistan's Intelligence Agency—with its own embedded Wahhabi sympathizers—to offer ISIS their ultimate dream: a nuclear weapon that could become the mother of all suicide bombs.

2

CLARITY IN CHAOS

Doctrines are meant to serve man, not the other way around.

—Amin Maalouf

"Uncle Terenzio, I don't understand . . ." my niece Fioretta asked me one day. Her eyes were full of worry. "Can you please explain ISIS? What is happening? Why are they attacking us? I have some friends who are so afraid."

"Of course," I said, calming her. "Next week, let's all meet and I'll tell you what I know."

This book began that day. I was in Italy at the time. My Florentine niece, Fioretta, asked me to speak about the Middle East. She said there was a lot of confusion among her friends, all sixteen-year-olds, and they simply wanted to understand what was behind the deaths, the chaos, and the terrorism.

Fioretta knew that I had grown up in Saudi Arabia, Iran, and Egypt. In fact, I had spent over thirty years in that immense region on the Mediterranean shores which extends south to the Gulf states of Kuwait, Bahrain, Qatar, and the Emirates. I sensed her bewilderment and agreed to talk about it all.

Surprisingly, the day before our meeting, her father called me and asked if a few others could sit in as well. Naturally, I said yes. When the day came, I entered the library and was stunned to see the room packed with seventy people: teenagers, their parents, and even grandparents! At that moment, I realized how deep their desire to understand the current crisis in the Middle East was.

It was this outpouring of concern that gave birth to these pages.

I felt compelled to explain the source of the anarchy. But, instead of talking about Syria or Afghanistan or Iraq, I began speaking about the small Wahhabi sect in Saudi Arabia. The room fell quiet.

"Rarely do you hear blame being laid at the feet of the Saudis," I said. But this "ally in the War on Terror" has been, quite simply, a primary source of ISIS ideology and foreign fighters. Many experts insist that Saudi Arabian and Qatari foundations and private funders have plowed money and arms into the Syrian civil war, much of it ending up in the hands of ISIS and other jihadi groups. The irony becomes more heightened when one reflects that our Western funds that purchase Saudi and Qatari oil daily also help to sustain ISIS. So, our compliance is a key to the conundrum.

I projected a map of Saudi Arabia that illustrated the country's different interpretations of Islam—on the eastern Gulf coast live a large population of Shias; along the western Hejaz on the Red Sea dwell a more relaxed strain of Sunnis. But in the central desert, the dominant puritanical Wahhabi doctrine is deeply rooted, and the clerics have privileged access to the purse strings as only their austere creed is recognized as the national faith.

I then explained how Saudi royal family members are all sworn followers to this doctrine and, over decades, billions of petrodollars have been directed into the proclaimed "Wahhabi mission" (*Dawa Wahhabiyya*) sending out proselytizing missionaries worldwide to convert other Muslims to adopt the Saudi creed and sharia legal code and, ultimately, their way of life. The Wahhabi mission operates across the Middle East and North Africa, Afghanistan, Pakistan, and Central Asia, as well as Malaysia, Indonesia, and, of course, in Europe—Kosovo, Bosnia, Albania, Belgium, France, and the UK. Support has come from the Saudi government; the royal family; Saudi charities; and Saudi-sponsored organizations including the World Muslim League, the World Assembly of Muslim Youth, and the International Islamic Relief Organization, providing the hardware of impressive edifices and the software of preaching and teaching.

I described how I've often heard my Arab friends lament that this rigid, fundamentalist culture has now crashed like a tsunami across the tolerant, diverse, and cosmopolitan Middle East with its uncompromising zealous vision to transform Islam, to radicalize traditional Muslims with the Wahhabi doctrine. In short, to Wahhabize the Sunni World.

The great conundrum for most moderate Muslims is that the two holy cities of Mecca and Medina have been in Wahhabi hands for ninety years. It is impossible to underestimate the symbolic prestige this brings the sect. In the nineteenth century, Wahhabism was confined only to rugged deserts in the Arabian Peninsula. Now it can be found throughout the Muslim world. In fact, the annual pilgrimage to Mecca, called the Hajj, now lies at the heart of global conversion as Saudis promote their doctrine to arriving pilgrims as the only "true Islam."

I narrated how the Wahhabi sect has profited greatest with non-Arabic speaking Muslims: Malaysians, Indonesians, and Pakistanis. Such pilgrims remain deeply impressed and offer unquestioning respect to the Wahhabis in their role as custodians of Mecca. Some even adopt the new creed out of insecurity when faced with proselytizing Saudis who claim that Allah has not heard their prayers because their practices are not correct. Southeast Asians are often followers of the liberal Sha'afi school. But, by accepting financial gifts for conversion, they must turn their backs on their ancestors' Sufi mystical Islam that originally came to their countries. Upon returning home, they start *madrasas* with Saudi money, cover their young daughters in hijab, and conform to the Saudi culture that they have witnessed in Mecca.

I then pointed out how this drama now touches us all. This small Wahhabi sect with its new doctrine has oversized reach and power. It now threatens the very soul of mainstream Islam. And, most shockingly, all the infamous terrorist groups today—from ISIS and al-Qaeda to Boko Haram and the Taliban—adhere to the Wahhabi sect's view of Islam. The question is why? What does Wahhabism offer that attracts such violent followers? My question hung in the air before I offered an answer.

In short, Wahhabis believe they have the divine right to condemn (*takfir*) or excommunicate any "impure" Muslims who do not follow their Wahhabi literalist line. They dismiss all others as *kafirs,* or non-believers. Shias, Yazidis, Alawites, Ismailis are all seen as apostates or heretics, along with other Sunnis from the four major schools, as well. Non-Muslims—Christians, Jews, Buddhists, and Hindus—are also included in this blanket condemnation. In this sect's uniquely intolerant doctrine, Wahhabi followers can not only condemn any traditional Muslims as "betrayers," but they are religiously sanctioned to also kill them and plunder their property.

This is the shocking truth. Embedded in the Wahhabi creed is the green light to judge, condemn, and commit violence against any non-believer. This creed—now exported outside of Saudi Arabia—has fueled Salafi movements around the world and lies at the heart of the jihadi extremist violence today.

As I continued, the crowd's attention grew. This is the secret key to explaining all the random bloodshed from Paris to Syria, from Yemen to Libya, from Iraq to Pakistan. Through the Wahhabi jihadist optic, each victim—Muslim and non-Muslims alike—is an apostate, to be eliminated with no pity, no remorse. The savage attacks on helpless, impoverished Yazidi villagers north of Mosul in Iraq—where ISIS fighters massacred the men and seized their women as sex slaves—are a case in point. ISIS leaders openly justified these acts as divine vengeance using the Wahhabi doctrine. Just seventy years ago, true believers in the Waffen SS dispatched Jews, Slavs, and Roma with the same conviction of purifying the world.

I then read the words of Professor Madawi al-Rashid, a Saudi Arabian social anthropologist interviewed by the BBC on December 19, 2015 for an article entitled "Is Saudi Arabia to Blame for the Islamic State?" She confirmed: "Wahhabism is definitely an intolerant form of Islam. It is a local religious tradition that has gone global prematurely. We're seeing that it can be a revolutionary language that would inspire someone to commit atrocities in the name of Islam."

I then continued with the words of Lebanese American Bernard Haykel, professor of Near Eastern Studies at Princeton University, who stated in his BBC interview "ISIS Theology Directly Linked to Wahhabism" on that same day: "Now, ISIS claims that the Saudi state has deviated from the true beliefs of Abdul Wahhab, and that they are the true representatives of the Salafi or Wahhabi message."

So, both ISIS and Saudi Arabia proclaim that they are the true heirs of the Wahhabi creed. And while they now openly condemn each other—ISIS leaders have called for the royal family's overthrow, while Saudi leaders have tired of ISIS's attacks and violence directed at Saudi Arabia—many observers miss a dramatic point: all that the Islamic State or ISIS has done is strictly apply the Wahhabi doctrine that was exported from Saudi Arabia and then adapt it for extremist, violent purposes.

After explaining all this, I ended my talk. The packed audience slowly began to rise, speaking animatedly among themselves. A concerned publisher came up and asked me to write a book on the subject. Then, my eyes fell on Fioretta still sitting in the front row with her young classmates. And to understand more, I offered to take her on a journey through Saudi Arabian culture, where it all began.

ARABIA OF THE WAHHABIS

The real question is how much suffering we've caused our womenfolk by turning headscarves into symbols—and using women as pawns in a political game.

—Orhan Pamuk

SPRING 2016

"But, what was it like to grow up in Saudi Arabia?" Fioretta asked.

"Well," I replied, "it was a bit different."

"How so?"

"It was surreal. I spent my early childhood in Dhahran, a large oil camp created for the employees and families of the great oil company ARAMCO, the Arabian American Company, where my father worked."

"And outside?"

"It was another world. There were different rules."

I described to Fioretta that I grew up in the heated deserts of eastern Saudi Arabia that border the placid Gulf waters. Inside this pioneer oil camp modeled on Arizona-style suburbia, my three brothers and I played on green lawns, softball fields, and in swimming pools; ate at snack bars selling milkshakes and hamburgers; and snuck into the movie theater to see the latest Hollywood epics.

Meanwhile, outside the gates of ARAMCO—Arabian American Oil Company—lay another world. Barren, tawny desert sands stretched to the far horizon. In this land, rules were different. Music and dance were banned, beer and wine were prohibited, and women were covered in black veils from head to toe. The town of Dammam lay nearby. A scattering of palm-lined oasis villages dotted this arid province called Al-Hasa and would surface like mirages on the dusty roads. Two separate worlds co-existing schizophrenically.

In the dusty souks of Dammam and Qatif, at high noon, shops always closed shut for noon prayers. As the doors were closing one day, I remember watching as an old bearded man lift his thin cane and then he reached out to strike two passing young girls across their ankles. They screamed and ran.

"What's he doing?" I asked my father.

"He's a *mutawa*," he told me. "A religious police."

"But why is he hitting those girls?"

"Too much exposed ankle."

These bearded volunteers eagerly patrolled the souks and any public places where men and women mixed. They acted with great relish, and their canes, followed by verbal assaults, got the message across. Ladies, be warned—dress appropriately or else.

On another souk visit, I remember my mother shaking her head with sadness as a *mutawa* admonished at a young teenager. More than once, I remember her describing it very clearly to me.

"Terry, it's a war against women," she would say.

My mother, Donna, hailed from Hutchinson, Kansas in conservative Midwestern America. Although she traveled into the traditional Arab world—from Egypt's languid Nile Valley to the impressive towering cedars in the Lebanese mountains—she had never seen this exaggerated form of policing and persecution of women. Only in Saudi Arabia was it law, deeply embedded in the culture and strictly enforced.

Legally, Saudi women are *not* free. They are legal possessions, bound by their male guardian, who may be their father, brother or husband. It is their guardian's role to make the final decision on the woman's key life choices. A woman may travel only if her guardian approves. She may work in a job only if her guardian approves. She can attend university only if her guardian approves. His signature is required for any of these choices. And, of course, women had long been prohibited from driving. Strangely, the actual religious interpretation was protective—it had been ruled that women may become aroused during driving and this may put them in danger. The same logic also applied to bicycle riding in the Kingdom, which was until recently prohibited to women. But the irony is that this conservative gender-apartheid is not inscribed in the Koran. It is simply an interpretation imposed by the Wahhabi sect.

Fioretta could not believe what she was hearing. Her eyes stared forcefully, as she asked more questions.

I told her that after my childhood in Saudi Arabia, and later Iran and Egypt, I returned to the Middle East to work as a cultural consultant. For ten years I was based in Athens, commuting across the Gulf in a region that was quickly mushrooming with new industries and banking, yet with small national populations. In all these Gulf countries, rapid growth required importing thousands of foreign skilled workers and professionals. These companies were globalized before the term even came into vogue.

In the 1980s, this blend of global cultures and languages created Towers of Babel—full of misunderstandings, chaos, and inefficiencies. The awkward mix included Japanese, French, Saudis, Brits, Yanks, Greeks, Egyptians, Palestinians, and Lebanese all reluctantly thrown together in golden-cocoon Arabian city-states, sprinkled on shifting sands and pounded by the blazing sun. My cultural consulting role was to act as a mediator, a diplomat; to unravel the cultural miscommunications, while building effective management teams.

It was during my assignments in Saudi Arabia that I witnessed firsthand the Wahhabi sect again and have returned often since then. Each visit brought back many memories.

I told Fioretta that Saudi Arabia today definitively remains a "man's world." Co-education does not exist; all classes are divided between the sexes. The fear of mixing women with men is dramatic. Meanwhile, women still scurry through enclosed marble shopping malls, keeping their exposed ankles one step ahead of the dreaded *mutawas*, the religious police. This gender-apartheid state has no equal on earth.

When I returned, the sound of wind on a tent flap had been replaced by the perpetual hum of air conditioning. Cases of pneumonia brought on by the artificial chill reached epidemic levels in summer. Social life and entertainment had been reduced to marathon video viewing. The ancient Bedouin culture of Arabia had traded in its camels for Cadillacs, gained a huge waistline and an obsession for Louis XV furniture, and, somewhere along that superhighway to the modern age, lost its charm and mortgaged its soul.

During a visit to Riyadh, I told Fioretta, I also witnessed "chop-chop square," where executions take place on Friday, the holy day. One afternoon I ventured past Deera Square where a large crowd had gathered. I moved in for a closer view. The spectators stood behind a line of soldiers. Of course, it was an all-male affair. I peered between the standing men.

In the center of the square, the executioner raised his sword above a crouched figure in white. The blade lifted high up, then swung back down sweeping away the condemned victim's head.

For murder and apostasy, summary executions are carried out, like the one I witnessed. Harsh Saudi laws also apply for persons caught stealing—amputation of the hand. Any behavior considered to be "un-Islamic" is rewarded with public shaming—the lash of the whip.

I told Fioretta's friends that few have noted how ISIS eagerly adopted and applied these uniquely Saudi punishments. From their capital of Raqaa in eastern Syria, the media-savvy techies turned their executions into terror-videos and unleashed a stream on You-Tube for the world to witness. They nodded silently.

After lunch, I described the lives of the legions of lowly paid expatriate Asian workers who are treated bleakly. Countless Bengalis,

Pakistanis, Filipinos, and Indians keep the economy afloat laboring in often shocking conditions. Some even quietly speak of a "slave state." All know that any complaints will mean the end of their jobs.

With their hard labor and an unending flow of petro-wealth, these workers have transformed these barren deserts into modern high-rise cities adorned with shopping malls sporting high-end luxury goods, fashion and cars. Not unlike Las Vegas, Porsches and BMWs are plentiful. Saudi women take pictures with their iPhones and share their images on Twitter and WhatsApp, which is revolutionizing the conservative kingdom. Valuable jeweled bracelets with precious stones and gold often cover the arms of ladies who may well be wearing designer clothes underneath their head-to-toe black *abayah* cloaks.

During my consulting assignments, I was often surprised to discover firsthand the depth of Wahhabi hatred for the Shias. In a casual conversation, one manager in ARAMCO's Security Department once whispered in confidence to me about the Shia working in the company: "You know, they're devil worshippers. We can't trust them."

"What do you mean?" I asked surprised. "They've virtually built this company."

"Just look from behind," he counseled me, "and you'll see their tails. Touch their heads, you can feel horns. One day soon, their time will come."

I could not believe I was hearing this from a university educated professional. After all, the Shia minority—who make up 15 percent of the Saudi population—are in a majority in the eastern province of Al-Hasa. The great irony is that the vast pools of petroleum reserves lie under these Saudi Shias' land, and yet all those riches flow straight to the Wahhabi capital of Riyadh with little benefits given to the Shia minority.

My father's best friends were Ahmad Al-Jafari and Ali Al-Hasa, young men from the nearby oases of Qatif and Saihat. When he mentored them, he sent Ahmad to Berkeley to master English. Later they both rose up the company career ladder to become leading managers in ARAMCO. But there was a glass ceiling for the Shia. Everyone knew that senior management posts were always reserved for Wahhabi appointees from the Nejd desert. The Shia were officially tolerated and numbered the largest group of employed Saudis, but seen as an undesirable and heathen minority by Riyadh. And yet, all the oil fields lay under their ancestral lands of Al-Hasa.

Over the years, I heard stories of the regime's persecution of the Shias that mirrored *Mississippi Burning*. It was a deep racism that rivaled the odious bigotry in America's Deep South. It was not rational. And there was no logical discussion possible. It is so ingrained that the "Shia heretics" were rendered satanic. Not unlike the accused Jews and Muslims during the Spanish Inquisition.

On the other hand, my younger brother Richard had also worked in ARAMCO as an Environmental Manager. He had heard similar strange things. One day, in 1998, his department colleague confided in him; Muhammad announced he planned to take his vacation to Afghanistan. Rich was stunned. After years of civil war, the country was devastated. It seemed like the last place on earth you would want to take a family holiday.

"Muhammad, are you crazy?" Richard asked. "With your family?"

"Of course, Rich," Muhammad replied. "The government is paying for our trip! We're going to see the *true* Islam."

Rich was surprised to hear that this government-sponsored trip was conceived so that Saudis could personally witness Taliban-run Afghanistan, the second Wahhabi imperial project. When Muhammad returned after a month in Kabul, he was ecstatic. He told Rich that the regime had taken as its model the society back home in Riyadh.

In fact, while the Saudi Kingdom pumped money into Kabul, the Taliban imposed draconian restrictions on women, shut down schools, destroyed Shia shrines, and banned music, TV, radio, and dance.

Then they turned to the colossal carved Buddha statues that stood for millennia as silent sentinels in the Bamiyan Valley. Before the advent of Islam, Buddhist culture had once thrived in Afghanistan. The legendary kingdom of Gandhara left a mark so deep that even the disciples of Allah who entered this mountainous land in the ninth century made no attempt to disturb these monuments for 1,200 years.

Fioretta was shocked to hear how, in March 2001, the Taliban began firing a barrage of anti-aircraft guns at the giant Buddhas in the cliffs. Applying Wahhabi logic that forbids idolatry, they blasted away for over a month, then they set dynamite to obliterate all traces. And these explosions were filmed. It was even rumored that phone calls were made to Riyadh to share the news and ensure that promised funds would be transferred. Overnight, these enduring symbols of Afghanistan's multi-cultural past were erased. And the world watched this strange sight played day after day on the news.

Abdul Salam Zaeef, the former Taliban Ambassador to Pakistan, described in his memoir, *My Life with The Taliban*, that Japan had offered to "cover the statues from head to toe in a way that no one would recognize they had ever been there, while preserving them underneath." He also recalled a Buddhist delegation from Sri Lanka that offered to dismantle the sculptures and re-assemble them far from danger. But no, they had to be destroyed.

I then told Fioretta how, in 2012, the fabled city of Timbuktu in the Sahara was overrun by Islamist fighters of al-Qaeda. Ahmad Al Mahdi led a morality brigade during the occupation and launched a campaign to erase all traces of what the jihadists considered un-Islamic idolatry. They ransacked sites where saints were venerated, destroying with pickaxes nine mausoleums and then blowing up the sacred door at Sidi Yahya mosque. All but one of the artifacts were on UNESCO's list of World Heritage sites. Timbuktu had long been known as the "city of 333 saints" from its ancient Sufi tradition. But, there was a glimmer of hope, I told Fioretta, Mr. Al Mahdi was now in the Hague, charged as the first defendant by the International Criminal Court for demolishing religious buildings and historical monuments, "a war crime under international law."

In 2014, ISIS had done the same at Queen Zenobia's classical city of Palmyra. In Mosul, they followed up by blasting the Nabi Tunis Mosque with its tomb of the Prophet Jonah, celebrated in the Koran, the Bible, and the Torah. They also destroyed the Virgin Mary Church along with numerous Shia mosques and shrines. Then the world watched in horror as videos streamed showing ISIS fighters smashing Mosul Museum's ancient artifacts and Assyrian statues with sledgehammers.

As true iconoclasts, Wahhabis do not accept reverence of any shrines or sacred figures. There can be no other source of the divine except Allah. This unified vision is the central focus of their doctrine. All else is idolatry, or *shirk*. Ancient historical sites across the Middle East and Asia were now at risk.

"Just think of Egypt's timeless Pharaonic temples along the Nile," I told Fioretta, "or the stunning tombs in Luxor or the crouching Sphinx facing Giza, or Lebanon's Temple of Bacchus at Baalbeck or Jordan's hidden pearl of Petra. Not to mention the myriad of early Christian monasteries dotted across Syria, many of which are now in ruins, thanks to the jihadists."

Yet, no journalists have ever reported that all these desecrations have been linked by the Wahhabi doctrine. No one speaks of this hidden connection. Why? The world stands bewildered at how, in the twenty-first century, we've witnessed an orgy of destruction of cultural patrimony and religious objects, erasing our collective past.

"But, aren't there any Saudis who are upset with their links with ISIS?" Fioretta asked me.

I told her about one former imam of the Grand Mosque in Mecca, Sheikh Adil al-Kalbani who spoke frankly in a TV interview on MBC Dubai what many in Saudi Arabia would not say. He openly declared that ISIS leaders used Wahhabi texts and "draw their ideas from what is written in our own books, our own principles."

I then told Fioretta's friends, if one just takes a close look at the education system of the Islamic State, all the signs are there. For instance, when ISIS fighters entered newly captured Syrian towns and Iraqi villages, they burned the old secular schoolbooks. Starting with a clean slate, they gave the shell-shocked students fresh new textbooks, all imported from Saudi Arabia. The Saudi Wahhabi curriculum was soon being taught in classrooms across the Islamic State—the fourth Wahhabi imperial project.

Then, ISIS branched into publishing. Among the twelve books by Muslim scholars printed by the Islamic State, seven have been teachings of the eighteenth-century founder of the Saudi doctrine, Muhammad Abdul Wahhab.

Fioretta wanted to know more.

4
A PACT IN THE DESERT

Allah will support the just state even if it is led by unbeliev-
ers, but Allah will not support the oppressive state even if it
is led by believers.

—Ibn Taymiyyah

SPRING 2016

"And, Uncle, just who was Abdul Wahhab?" asked Fioretta.

"The founder of the Saudi doctrine." I answered.

"So Wahhabis follow him."

"That's right. Like the Lutherans follow Luther, and Calvinists follow Calvin."

"And they live in Arabia?" she asked.

"Yes, in the center, in the heart of the Nejd desert. Have a look at this map."

I pulled out a map and asked Fioretta and her friends to study it carefully. The light green marked the *Sunni* followers—Egypt, Jordan, Turkey, Afghanistan, and parts of Iraq and Syria. The dark green marked the *Shia* followers—Iran, parts of Yemen, Lebanon, Iraq and Bahrain. And then there was purple coloring in the center of Arabia.

"This," I explained, "is the heartland of the *Wahhabi*."

In the central Nejd desert, temperatures can peak at 110 degrees. In this unforgiving, barren landscape, Muhammad Abdul Wahhab (1703–1792) founded the sect that bears his name. He stressed the absolute sovereignty of God, *tawhid* or "God's unity," and rejected any veneration of saints, holy figures, or even the Prophet Muhammad. He declared the "cult of saints" as idolatry (*shirk*), although it had been practiced widely among Shia and Sufis for a thousand years. And he denounced pilgrimages to saints' tombs and destroyed these shrines.

His evangelizing in the Arabian Peninsula during the eighteenth century called for a return to the practices of the first converts to Islam. Any Muslims who disagreed with his definition of monotheism, he condemned (*takfir*) as apostates of Islam.

Yet, over the last millennium, diverse cultures had enriched Islamic civilization that stretched across the African and Asian continents to the distant South China Sea in a wide array of interpretations, beliefs and practices. Among Sunni followers, four major schools of religious law had emerged: Hanafi, Maliki, Sha'afi, and Hanbali. Both Ottoman and Moghul rulers had embraced the Hanafi school and diffused it across their empires. At the same time, Shia branches included the Jafari in Iran and Iraq, Ismaili in Pakistan, Alevi in Turkey, Ibadi in Oman, Zaidi in Yemen, Alawite in Syria, and the Druze in Lebanon.

Yet, Abdul Wahhab rejected all these interpretations of Islam. He declared that the faith had been polluted by cultural contamination under the Ottoman Empire and before. With striking zeal and

xenophobia, he accused his fellow Muslims of practicing "innovations" (*bida*). According to his doctrine, they were heretics.

Instead, he demanded a return to the "purity" of the Salaf: the
first generation of Islam. His political project aimed at bringing all
Muslims back to the original faith by establishing an Islamic political system, the *sharia*, set out in Koranic law interpreted through
his eyes.

His austere vision was deeply influenced by the teachings of Ibn
Taymiyyah, a scholar who lived in Damascus in the fourteenth
century during the Mongol invasions ravaging the Middle East.
Defiantly, Ibn Taymiyyah issued an Islamic legal ruling (*fatwa*)
excommunicating the converted Mongol invaders as apostates or
unbelievers (*kafirs*), even though they were indeed Muslims. And
then he sanctioned jihad against them. His ruling was anchored by
his accusation that the Mongols governed *without* Islamic law, but
by their tribal laws. Strikingly, Ibn Taymiyyah's religious *fatwa* was
the first that ever justified inter-Muslim violence. And, quite amaz-
ingly this ruling lies at the heart of Abdul Wahhab's doctrine.

Resurrecting Ibn Taymiyyah's ruling four hundred years later,
Abdul Wahhab found new "fallen Muslims" to condemn. In eastern Arabia, the Shia lived on palm-lined oases and revered their
saints: Ali and his sons Hussein and Hassan. In the Hejaz to the
West, numerous Sufis thrived in the cities of Mecca, Medina, and
Jeddah, revering their founding masters, chanting prayers in their
ceremonies to music, some even danced.

Abdul Wahhab not only excommunicated (*takfir*) these fellow
Muslims, but he granted his desert Bedouin followers the right to

kill them and loot their property. Using the conquistadors' logic in Latin America, the Bedouin warriors were empowered on a religious mission to attack the heretics and plunder at will. And so they did.

Like Martin Luther, the preacher Abdul Wahhab needed a political ally to spread his doctrine. His crucial moment came in 1744, when he was forty-one years old. A pact was forged with the tribal chieftain, Muhammad ibn Saud, founder of the Saud dynasty, in the small desert oasis of Diriyah (just outside today's capital of Riyadh) in central Arabia. This date marks the birth of the Saudi-Wahhabi state. From that year on, Abdul Wahhab's followers were bound to the family known today as the House of Saud.

Few Westerners know that one of the most shocking Wahhabi raids took place only a few years after Abdul Wahhab's death. In 1802, the Saud leader led an army of 10,000 Bedouin to attack the Iraqi city of Karbala. It was a slaughter of the innocents. This holy city was ransacked and plundered, its citizens put to the sword. Karbala had always been a pilgrimage site for Shia as it holds the revered shrine of Hussein, martyred grandson of the Prophet.

A Wahhabi chronicler and court historian, Uthman ibn Bishr, described the murder and pillaging with messianic zeal:

The Muslims scaled the walls, entered the city . . . and killed the majority of its people in the markets and in their homes. [They] destroyed the dome placed over the grave of Hussein [and took] whatever they found inside the dome and its surroundings . . . the grill surrounding the tomb which was encrusted with emeralds, rubies, and other jewels . . . different types of property, weapons, clothing, carpets, gold, silver, precious copies of the Qur'an.

The commander of the expedition, the grandson of Muhammad Ibn Saud, then wrote to the Ottoman governor in Iraq defending their actions:

As for your statement that we seized Karbala, slaughtered its people, and took their possessions—praise belongs to God, Lord of the Worlds! We make no apology for that, and we say: "And like catastrophes await the unbelievers" [Quran 47:10].

The following year, Wahhabi warriors also assaulted the western city of Ta'if in the Sarat Mountains above the Red Sea. Reports surfaced that they massacred the entire male population and sold the women and children into slavery.

Then, they shocked the Islamic world by attacking and subjugating the holy city of Mecca that was the center of the Sufi universe. In the chaos and the looting, the annual Hajj was disrupted. The Prophet's tombstone was destroyed in order to prevent fellow Muslims from "worshipping" it. Shrines were destroyed.

Finally, the enraged Sultan of Egypt, Muhammad Ali, dispatched his army to Yanbu, the port of Medina in 1813 and hurled the Wahhabi and their Saud leader back into the Nejd desert, finally destroying their capital of Diriyah and ending their threat for a century. Only then did the legendary Hashemite family that had ruled Mecca, return to the holy city.

But, a century later, in 1902, another Saud king, the young and aggressive Abdul-Aziz Ibn Saud rallied the descendents of the Wahhabi followers calling them the *Ikhwan* (the Brotherhood) to set out on a new conquest of Arabia. Ibn Saud hoped to forge a reliable source of an elite army corps. In order to break their tribal feuds, he settled the Bedouin in colonies called *hijrah*s in desert oases, offering them living quarters, mosques, schools, agricultural tools, arms and ammunition. Most importantly, religious teachers instructed the *Ikhwan* in the fundamentalist doctrine preached by Abdul Wahhab. And they became arch-traditionalists.

A decade later, Ibn Saud's army was ready. They first rode east, seizing the Shia region of Al-Hasa along the Gulf in 1913 from the reeling Ottomans. The Ikhwan tried to impose Wahhabism on the local Shia population and Wahhabi clerics issued a *fatwa* obliging the Shias to convert to the "true Islam."

Once the First World War broke out, conspiring British agents encouraged Ibn Saud to rebel against the Ottomans. An Anglo–Saud friendship treaty was signed and Saudi lands became a British protectorate. The treaty insisted that Ibn Saud respect Britain's Gulf protectorates—Kuwait, Qatar, and the Emirates—but it purposely neglected any word about the Sharifate of Mecca to the west. With Britain's blessing, Ibn Saud and his Wahhabis were left free to attack, occupy, and plunder the Holy City at a time of his choosing.

Meanwhile, Sharif Hussein bin Ali, heir of the tolerant and illuminated Hashemite family that had ruled Mecca and Medina for seven hundred years, had also allied with Britain. The Sharifs of Mecca had always served as the traditional stewards of the holy cities in the Hejaz along the Red Sea. *Sharif* means "noble" in Arabic and is used to describe the descendants of the Prophet, and this enlightened family had protected Mecca and Medina for thirty-seven generations as "custodians" over the centuries and ensured the safety of pilgrims.

At the height of World War I, Sharif Hussein proclaimed the great Arab Revolt against the Ottoman Empire, in which Lawrence of Arabia gained his fame. The British promised him full support for Arab independence and even offered the title "King of the Arabs." But, once the war ended, British and French diplomats at Versailles imposed colonial rule across Palestine, Syria and Iraq. Feeling spectacularly betrayed, Sharif Hussein refused to ratify the Versailles Treaty and the Anglo–Hashmite Treaty.

By 1924, *Ikhwan* warriors were galloping west on their camels. First, they laid siege to the Ta'if. Once the city fell, three hundred unprotected residents were massacred. Then, the *Ikhwan* invaded the sacred cities in the Hejaz that face the Red Sea. The iconoclast Wahhabis lopped the dome off the house of the Prophet in Medina, destroyed the cemetery of Jannat al-Baqi where the Prophet's daughter was buried, ransacked the treasuries of the holy places in Mecca, and plundered the port of Jeddah. Sharif Hussein appealed for help, but his call fell on deaf ears. His former British allies abandoned him to the Bedouins' wrath.

In this fateful moment of history, the British betrayed not only Sharif Hussein, but also the entire Islamic world by choosing to replace the tolerant, cosmopolitan custodian of Mecca with militant, puritanical Bedouins. This turn of events would have lasting consequences.

Sharif Hussein had no choice but to flee into exile, and later he would die in Jordan where his cosmopolitan great-grandson reigns today as King Abdullah, the last Hashemite ruler.

"Just imagine," I told Fioretta, "how different the world would be if they were still custodians of Mecca."

I then explained how Ibn Saud then proclaimed himself King of the Hejaz. For his loyalty and service to the British crown, Ibn Saud was awarded a knighthood, and is referred to as "Sir" in official documents.

To this day, some Arabs point to the British support of Ibn Saud—instead of the legitimate time-honored Hashemite family— as the pivotal act that led to the crisis within Islam now.

"The British," I told Fioretta, "chose a more obedient servant to guard the oil wells. And the Islamic world paid a terrible price." She nodded slowly with understanding.

Heady with their victories across much of the Arabian Peninsula, the *Ikhwan* become uncontrollable. Deeply suspicious of "modernity," they dismantled radio antennae and electricity poles, rejecting telephones and the telegraph. They demanded forced conversion or expulsion of the Shia in the Eastern Province. When Ibn Saud forbade new raiding, tensions finally boiled over.

In 1927, the *Ikhwan* openly rebelled. After two years of fighting, the uprising was crushed and the rebels were subdued. This brutal crackdown left long-simmering resentments between the ultra-conservative Wahhabis and the Saud royal family. Even today, the uneasy alliance between them still carries great tension.

Ibn Saud and his descendants understood the only way to reduce discontent was to grant the Wahhabis clerics religious and social control, in return for their loyalty. Only in 1962, did Wahhabi authorities allow slavery to be abolished. Two more years passed before women were allowed to go to school and televisions were allowed to enter homes.

In the 1970s, thanks to the generous flood of oil revenues, the royal family placated the religious establishment by unleashing Saudi charities to fund Wahhabi schools, missionaries, and mosques across the world. The Ministry of Religious Affairs proclaimed *Dawa Wahhabiyya* (the Wahhabi Mission) to spread "purified" Islam across the Muslim World to convert the apostates or *kafirs*.

When Soviet tanks rolled into Afghanistan in 1979, America searched for Muslim combatants to counter the communists in a guerilla insurgency. National Security Advisor, Zbigniew Brezinski, turned to his Saudi Arabian counterparts and encouraged them to send thousands of volunteers to fight in jihad against the atheist Soviet–backed Kabul regime. They eagerly complied with America's blessing.

This would be the grand finale to the Cold War, and the birth of many new ones.

SIEGES OF MECCA

I tell my brethren in Palestine: be patient and continue your
blessed struggle. We did not forget you. We are still healing
another wound in the Muslim nation, which is the occupa-
tion of our land by the Americans. Your battle and ours are
one and the same.

—MUHAMMAD OMAR, TALIBAN LEADER

SUMMER 2016

"Tell me more about Mecca, Uncle," Fioretta asked. "Do pilgrims continue to go to the city?"

"Absolutely," I said. "But it was in Mecca, in that same year of 1979, that the Saud family also faced its biggest crisis."

I began describing to Fioretta and her friends the siege of Mecca.

On November 20, armed militants openly rebelled and seized the Grand Mosque. Their leader, Juhayman Al-Otaybi, was a preacher. His grandfather had ridden with Ibn Saud and his other family members were considered legends among the *Ikhwan*. Juhayman brazenly called for the overthrow of the House of Saud, proclaiming that the ruling family was betraying Islamic principles and adopting a corrupt western lifestyle.

Juhayman and his followers were theology students from the University of Medina who had studied with Sheikh ibn Baz (who later was appointed the Grand Mufti of Saudi Arabia) and other leading clerics. The rebels ominously called themselves *Beit al-Ikhwan*, House of the Brotherhood.

Rattled by this shocking attack, King Khalid took no chances. He called Pakistan and France for outside help. Pakistani commandos with French Special Operations Forces—who required "momentary conversion" to enter the holy city and the mosque—put down the uprising. The two-week long siege ended with 250 dead. The rebels all perished by bullets or later by executioners' swords.

But Juhayman's courageous actions and fearless conviction struck a chord with the archconservatives across the country. The Saud family was reeling in shock, having been denounced as illegitimate and corrupt by Juhayman.

The royal family desperately appealed to the loyal Wahhabi establishment to condemn Juhayman's uprising. But, it came at a high cost. King Khalid did not crack down on dissidents because, after all, the accusations held some kernels of truth. In this moment of great vulnerability, the royal family ceded all control of education, religious affairs, and social behavior to the Wahhabi archconservatives. For King Khalid, the solution to this religious upheaval was simple: more religion.

Culture wars began anew against any tentative social reforms. Photos of women in newspapers were banned along with women on TV. Music stores and cinemas were shut down. School curriculums added many more hours of religious studies. Classes on non-Islamic history were eliminated. Gender segregation was enforced in even the humblest coffee shop. And the pipeline of funds for Wahhabi missionary projects flowed more plentiful than ever before.

This was a watershed moment: 1979.

Across the Gulf, a king had fallen—the Shah of Iran had fled his country. In his place, a religious cleric, Ayatollah Khomeini, seized power, proclaiming the Islamic Republic of Iran. In Saudi Arabia, the ultra-conservative religious forces gained complete control over Saudi society. Saudi Arabia and Iran, once allies and twin pillars of US strategy in the region, would become mortal enemies after 1979. It was all sparked by both the Siege of Mecca and the Iranian Revolution. Then, it was fueled by American policy. Juhayman may have died, but his dream lived on. The House of Saud allowed for his austere vision to be imposed across the country. And they exported it abroad, in grand competition with their Iranian rivals.

A colleague of mine, an imam in London, recalled how during that period, in the UK, the Saudis financed mosques and bought up all the publishing houses dealing with Islamic subjects. "Wahhabism follows strictly the letter of Sharia law, forgetting completely the spirituality of Islam," he said. "It obsesses only about *bida*, or innovation. In short, they have taken out the rituals that open the spiritual heart and treat the faith as if it belonged only to the Saudis, only to the Arabs. But, Islam is a universal faith that stretches beyond the Arabian Peninsula. Islam belongs to the world."

In Saudi Arabia, Ibn Baz and his conservative Wahhabi allies looked eagerly abroad to further spread their doctrine. They would use Mecca as their showpiece. And to do this, they had to sanitize the holy city of its past completely.

I shared with my niece the writings of Ziauddin Sardar, a leading authority on the Hajj and Mecca. Sadar helps explain what motivates the Wahhabi obsession with cultural obliteration. In his *New York Times* op-ed, "The Destruction of Mecca," he describes the clerics' "deep hatred of history. They want everything to look brand new . . . an amalgam of Disneyland and Las Vegas."

Sadar first witnessed the destruction in the mid-1970s when countless ancient buildings bulldozed to the ground, including the Bilal Mosque dating from the time of Prophet Muhammad. He cites the desecrations in detail:

> *The Makkah Royal Clock Tower, completed in 2012, was built on the graves of an estimated 400 sites of cultural and historical significance, including the city's few remaining millennium-old buildings. . . . The house of Khadijah, the first wife of the Prophet Muhammad, has been turned into a block of toilets. The Makkah Hilton is built over the house of Abu Bakr, the closest companion of the prophet and the first caliph.*
>
> *The only other building of religious significance in the city is the house where Prophet Muhammad lived. During most of the Saudi era it was used first as a cattle market, then turned into a library, which is not open to the people. But even this is too much for the radical Saudi clerics who have repeatedly called for its demolition. The clerics fear that, once inside, pilgrims would pray to the prophet, rather than to God—an unpardonable sin. It is only a matter of time before it is razed and turned, probably, into a parking lot.*

Needless to say, the shrines built for revered Sufi sheikhs no longer exist. As the Wahhabis feared that such places would become places of veneration, all historical traces were erased, even of the Prophet and his family.

For years, Wahhabi clerics have even had demanded the destruction of the fifteenth-century green dome that rests above the inscribed tomb holding the Prophet, Abu Bakr and Umar in Medina. The mosque is regarded as the second holiest site in Islam. A pamphlet published in 2007 by the Saudi Ministry of Islamic Affairs, endorsed by Abdulaziz Al Sheikh, the Grand Mufti of Saudi Arabia, stated that "the green dome shall be demolished and the three graves flattened in the Prophet's Masjid." Even the mountain cave where the Prophet received his Koranic revelations is today a site of veneration by many South Asian pilgrims. It too is being targeted. Hardliners have spoken about destroying the mountain altogether.

In the end, the Wahhabis in Saudi Arabia and ISIS share a fundamental worldview. Sadar bluntly calls it, "a hatred of the past."

"No one has the courage to stand up and condemn this cultural vandalism," says Dr. Irfan al-Alawi who, as executive director of the Islamic Heritage Research Foundation, has fought in vain to protect his country's historical sites. "We have already lost 400–500 sites. I just hope it's not too late to turn things around. We would never allow someone to destroy the pyramids, so why are we letting Islam's history disappear?"

Sami Angawi, renowned Saudi expert on the region's Islamic architecture and founder of the Jeddah-based Hajj Research Center has spent the last three decades documenting historic buildings of Mecca and Medina, few of which now remain. According to Dr.

Angawi as few as twenty structures are left that date back to the lifetime of the Prophet 1,400 years ago and those that remain could be bulldozed at any time. "This is the end of history in Mecca and Medina and the end of their future," describes Dr. Angawi. "At the root of the problem is Wahhabism. They have a big complex about idolatry and anything that relates to the Prophet." Born in Mecca, Angawi finally gave up and moved to Jeddah, where he now lives in a house designed in traditional Hejazi style.

Today, Muslims are still voicing concern, asking what is the meaning of religious pilgrimage if one cannot tread on traces of history, if one cannot view and touch the past?

Since that apocryphal year of 1979, many planted seeds have borne fruit. In recently leaked diplomatic memos, Hillary Clinton highlighted the success of wealthy, conservative Gulf donors in bankrolling the Afghan and Pakistani conflicts while their host governments have done little to stop them. Since the 1990s, the Grand Mufti of Saudi Arabia, Sheikh ibn Baz, had urged his countrymen to donate generously to the Taliban, whom he called heroic, pure, young Salafi warriors.

By December 2009, Secretary of State Hillary Clinton clearly understood where the money trail began. "Donors in Saudi Arabia constitute the most significant source of funding to Sunni terrorist groups worldwide. Saudi Arabia remains a critical financial support base for al-Qaeda, the Taliban, and Lashkar-e-Taiba (in Pakistan)."

Clinton's cables also give us insight into how donations were made. Pakistani militants slipped into Saudi Arabia disguised as pilgrims. There, they raised funds and created front companies to receive money from government-sanctioned charities.

One cable detailed how a Saudi-based front company funded the Pakistani group, Lashkar-e-Taiba, that launched the bloody Mumbai attacks in 2008. Officials of this group's charity wing traveled to Saudi Arabia to seek donations for new schools at vastly inflated costs—then siphoned off the money to fund their terrorist operations.

Clinton, in the same cable, described her Saudi allies as reluctant to stop this flow of funds. "It's an ongoing challenge to persuade Saudi officials to treat terrorist funds emanating from Saudi Arabia as a strategic priority." She then identified three Saudi charities, seen as terrorist entities in the US, which were still operating in the Kingdom. "Intelligence suggests that these groups continue to send money overseas and, at times, fund extremism overseas."

By July 2013, the European Parliament publically declared "Wahhabism as the main source of global terrorism." And, in another released email of a private conversation three months later, Clinton, allegedly said "the Saudis have exported more extreme ideology than any other place on Earth over the course of the last thirty years," during a closed-door speech to the Jewish United Fund in Chicago on October 28, 2013.

Meanwhile, the Saudi ruling family still applauded and promoted Wahhabism for its piety and the movement's strident opposition the regional ambitions of Iran and Shia communities in the Arab world.

Recently, the US State Department has estimated that over the past four decades Riyadh has invested more than ten billion dollars into charitable foundations in its attempt to Wahhabize mainstream Sunni Islam. European Union intelligence experts estimated that from this sum between 15 to 20 percent has been diverted to al-Qaeda and other violent jihadists.

In the end, the roots of the crisis may be the exclusive thoughts of Ibn Taymiyyah and Abdul Wahhab that justify the use of violence by ISIS and al-Qaeda. Jihadists have carried out attacks inside and outside Saudi Arabia. From atrocities in Paris, bombings in Brussels and Beirut, attacks in London, Manchester, Nice, and Berlin, to suicide bombings in Shia mosques in eastern Saudi Arabia, that ideology remains the same.

Instead of focusing on these uncomfortable links, the Anglo American media eagerly reports on social reforms in Saudi Arabia under the new King Salman. The sound of music, which once might have led to imprisonment, now can be heard on the radio. Minarets for mosques and use of funeral markers, which were once forbidden, are allowed. Prayer attendance, once enforced by flogging, is no longer obligatory. And to big fanfare, women were recently given the right to vote and drive. Meanwhile, the Saudi government hired public relations groups en masse for a concerted media campaign to enhance the image of Saudi Arabia.

However, in the end, the truth remains. Wahhabis still view all other non-Wahhabis in the same light. They still refer to those outside their sect as "nonbelievers." Those foreign fighters waving the black flags of ISIS proudly embraced the Wahhabi doctrine. Just look at the title of the ISIS publication, "Sheikh Baghdadi in the Footsteps of Imam Muhammad ibn Abdul

Wahhab: The Resemblance Between the Wahhabi and Baghdadi States."

Ironically, Prophet Muhammad and his beloved son-in-law Ali warned against the rise of extremism in *Kitab Al Fitan*—a compilation of *hadiths* (Islamic tradition) relating to the end of times. It was all compiled in 851 by the prominent scholar Nuyam bin Hammad. In this *hadith*, Ali recalls the Prophet saying:

> *If you see the black flags, then hold your ground and do not move your hands or your feet. A people will come forth who are weak and have no capability, their hearts are like blocks of iron. They are the people of the State, they do not keep a promise or a treaty. They call to the truth, but they are not its people. Their names are the names of cities,* (like the Caliph of ISIS al-Baghdadi,) *and their hair is loose like women's hair. They fight among themselves, then Allah will bring the truth.*

With these words, the Prophet seems to describe the ISIS onslaught.

"You may want to ask," I told Fioretta and her friends, "why the American media is still reluctant to draw the clear link between ISIS, Wahhabism, and Saudi Arabia. It's obvious that journalists and politicians don't want to connect the dots."

I pointed out again that ISIS soldiers who carried out attacks in Europe and America had Saudi connections, as did all the al-Qaeda hijackers on 9/11. In London, the Westminster attacker Khalid Masood was radicalized while teaching English in Saudi Arabia, just as the Pakistani couple of the San Bernadino shooting rampage in Southern California were radicalized during visits there.

Not understanding the radical Wahhabi doctrine, the Trump administration placed a travel ban on eight Muslim nations while ignoring the most glaring candidate. After all, wealthy Saudi princes and tycoons have purchased apartments in Trump properties. And their money has bought deafening silence ever since 9/11.

I could tell Fioretta was getting agitated.

UNSPOKEN CONNECTIONS

Jihad is becoming as American as apple pie and as British as afternoon tea.

—ANWAR AL-AWLAKI, AMERICAN IMAM

SUMMER 2016

"But, Uncle, if the Saudis were involved in 9/11," asked Fioretta, "why did the Americans invade Iraq?"

"That is the most important question." I replied. "The American media believed Bush's fabricated lie about Saddam's involvement . . . about the weapons of mass destruction."

I explained how fifteen of the nineteen hijackers were Saudis, as was Osama bin Laden. But the face of the story was one Egyptian, Mohamed Atta. Few knew that he also traveled on a Saudi passport. In the end, the faces of the other Saudis were rarely revealed. People only spoke about the sultry-eyed Egyptian.

Money fueled Bin Laden's operations. If America wanted to attack the regimes that supported Bin Laden, how could numerous influential and moneyed Saudi citizens escape the charge? For years, the export and proselytizing of the Wahhabi message deflected internal criticism in Saudi Arabia of royal corruption, decadence and American dependence.

After the first Gulf War in 1991, it became chic to criticize the royals in private. Conspiracy theories were rife. Most Saudis were convinced that the elder President Bush gave Saddam Hussein the green light to invade Kuwait so that he could place American GIs on Saudi soil.

Some xenophobic Saudis called it the "great betrayal" and never forgave the royal family for allowing "the holy land" to be desecrated.

From that moment, Bin Laden publicly condemned the ruling Saudi royals as corrupt tyrants to be overthrown. This is not new. Militant anti-imperialist strains of political Islam have roots in recent history—from the Mahdi's victory over "Gordon of Khartoum" in 1885 which shocked Victorian England, to Egypt's Muslim Brotherhood of Hassan al-Bannah in the 1920's created to expel the British, and later the Islamic Revolution that hurled the Shah and America out of Iran in 1979. Even the failed rebels who seized Mecca's Great Mosque in the same year were actors in that long tradition.

Bin Laden called for the royal family to cast the infidels out of the Prophet's sacred land. He dreamed of an Islamic theocratic state. He hoped to drive the heathen American soldiers off Saudi soil. His call resonated throughout the Gulf. In response, over the years, Gulf Arabs wired money to the elusive accounts of his al-Qaeda organization.

Like the romantic Lawrence of Arabia and the Bedouins who blew up the Hejaz Railroad of the imperialist Ottomans during the First World War, Bin Laden's strike in New York rang with symbolism for Saudi dissidents and across the Gulf. And after the strike, the Americans quietly moved their military bases to Qatar.

The final Senate report on 9/11 excluded twenty-eight pages of evidence about Saudi Arabia's connections to the hijackers. The pages were jealously guarded, for "security reasons," until this year, when they were released with a few censored passages. The pages revealed what we have known for a long time: Saudis officials *had* assisted some hijackers with funds once they came to America. After all, two hijackers had the phone number of the Aspen office of the Saudi ambassador to Washington, Bandar bin Sultan al-Saud.

Only now are lawsuits being brought against the Saudi government in American courts by families of those lost in 9/11. They declare that a network of the kingdom's officers, employees, and/or agents met with and aided the hijackers, providing them with money, cover, advice, contacts, transportation, assistance with language and US culture, identification, access to pilot training, and other material support. (On May 13, 2020, we finally learned the name of a Saudi diplomat, Mussaed al-Jarrah, who directed assistance given to two of the 9/11 hijackers. The FBI mistakenly disclosed Mr. al-Jarrah's name in its response to the lawsuit by the 9/11 families. Attorney General Barr was not pleased and filed motions with the court saying that any information relating to the Saudi embassy official were sensitive state secrets.)

The security reason for excluding these pages, however, was critical. If the Saudi identities in the operation had been highlighted, how could George Bush stand on his claim that Saddam Hussein and Iraqis—not Saudi Arabians—were behind the destruction of the Twin Towers? That was why redacting the report was crucial— so that he could attack Iraq and leave his Saudi allies in peace.

The Americans, with their servile British ally Tony Blair, lobbied the UN heavily speaking of an imaginary arsenal of mass destruction in the hands of Saddam. With that fabrication and deceit, the American forces massed in Kuwait, invaded Iraq, and quickly occupied Baghdad. Shortly after, Paul Bremer, Bush's Presidential Envoy to Iraq, dismissed the entire Iraqi Army overnight on May 16, 2003 labeling them "Baathists." This staggeringly naive blunder left tens of thousands of Sunni soldiers without a job. All returned to their homes, with no way to support their families. They also carried their weapons. Then, the firebrand President Maliki was elected by the Shia majority and backed by the Americans. For Maliki, it was time to correct the Shia suffering of the past. Overnight, he launched his vendetta against the Sunni "Baathists" who had earlier governed under Saddam.

During the first years of occupation, thousands of Sunni ex-soldiers and civilians were rounded up, and imprisoned in the notorious Abu Ghraib and Camp Bucca, run by the American forces. These brutal, humiliating torture centers inadvertently became the prime training grounds for future leaders and jihadists of ISIS. The world of Saddam had fallen. And these hardened soldiers eagerly embraced a new flag with a new Islamic identity. The Wahhabi lens viewed all Shia as heretics. This optic served them well. As *takfiri* warriors, they would take revenge.

Forming into cells of "al-Qaeda in Iraq," these enraged ex-prisoners launched a terror campaign of car bombings and suicide attacks. The Sunni insurgency began in full force. Gulf countries, foundations, and private citizens, startled by a Shia majority ruling Baghdad with Iranian support, offered generous funding to Sunni insurgents. As Saudi Arabia refused to recognize Maliki's Iraqi government, Gulf money began to clandestinely fund "al-Qaeda in Iraq" who turned their guns on the new Iraqi regime and the American occupiers.

I then shared with Fioretta a surreal story. My friend Neil Mac-Farquhar, who was the *New York Times* correspondent for the Middle East, recounted to me one of his meetings with a radicalized jihadist that he interviewed in Beirut. This young Lebanese man told Neil that he was so full of anger and humiliation about the American occupation in Iraq that he traveled there to volunteer as a suicide bomber. Once he got to Baghdad, he was taken to a secret room filled with young men. Upon entering, he boldly announced to the boss he was ready to die as a martyr. But then he was firmly told to take a number, sit down and wait. There was a line of many others before him.

"I was furious and yelled, 'You think I've come all this way to wait?! I don't have time to waste.'" he said.

"What happened then?" Neil asked.

"I told them all to go to hell and left slamming the door!" His hand hit the table for effect. "Three days later, I was back in Beirut."

Fioretta looked at me wide-eyed in disbelief.

I then said, "But, this gives you some idea of how deep the humiliation was felt across the Arab world."

When the Arab Spring erupted in Tunisia in 2010, it quickly spread to Egypt. By March 2011, demonstrators gathered in the southwestern Syrian town of Daraa. Assad's soldiers opened fire into the crowd igniting a civil war. Syrian Sunni rebels soon received substantial funding and arms from private donors in Saudi Arabia and Qatar hoping to depose Assad whose family were Alawites, a sect of Shia. The Saudis sent out the call that Assad must go, and foreign Sunni jihadis flocked to join the battle. Then, Hezbollah fighters from Lebanon and Shia soldiers from Iran joined in backing Assad. The conflict blew out of control.

Soon, "al-Qaeda in Iraq" seized their opportunity: the Sunni ex-generals, colonels, and officers of Saddam's defeated military crossed the border into Syria to join in the battle. "Al-Qaeda in Iraq" then changed its name to ISIS (Islamic State of Iraq and Syria).

ISIS then captured a large city—Raqqa in the east. Soon after, Mosul fell to a few thousand fighters. The fearful Iraqi Army abandoned the northern city once known as Nineveh. And it was in Mosul that on July 5, 2014, that Abu Bakr al-Baghdadi, an ex-prisoner of Camp Bucca in Iraq, emerged from the shadows to lead Friday prayers at Mosul's Great Mosque. He called on the world's Muslims to "obey" him as the head of the caliphate that been declared only a week before in late June. The last time such a pan-Muslim government had been seen was under the Ottoman Empire.

In October 2, 2014, Vice President Joe Biden giving a lecture at Harvard's Kennedy School described the Syrian tragedy at Harvard's Kennedy School:

> *My constant cry is that our biggest problem was our allies. . . . The Turks, the Saudis, the Emirates, etc., they were so determined to take down Assad and essentially have a proxy Sunni-Shia war. What did they do? They poured hundreds of millions of dollars and thousands of tons of weapons into anyone who would fight against Assad. Except that the people who were being supplied were Al-Nusra and al-Qaeda and the extremist elements of jihadis coming from other parts of the world. You think I'm exaggerating take a look. . . . And we could not convince our colleagues to stop supplying them.*

Hillary Clinton, in a recently leaked confidential email, echoed the same lament that same year. "We need to use our diplomatic and more traditional intelligence assets to bring pressure on the governments of Qatar and Saudi Arabia, which are providing clandestine financial and logistic support to ISIL and other radical Sunni groups in the region."

In confidence, an Arab American friend who worked in northern Saudi Arabia during that time related to me that his Saudi driver told him that he was offered $20,000 a month to go and fight in Syria. His package also included a $200,000 signing bonus and full life insurance coverage for his family if he did not return home. He turned down the offer.

By October 2015, the *New York Times* editorial "Why Is Money Still Flowing to ISIS?" repeated the concern a year later, highlighting that businessmen, wealthy families, and private donors from Saudi Arabia, Qatar, and Kuwait were still channeling donations to the Islamic State. By summer 2016, a few journalists began to probe deeper into the unspoken connection.

Ben Hubbard, a correspondent for the *New York Times* examined in his article, "Secrets of the Kingdom: A Fundamentalist Creed," how the Wahhabi doctrine is viewed by other Muslims.

While Wahhabism has adherents around the world, many Muslims detest it, because it considers Shiites and followers of other non-Sunni sects—not to mention Christians and Jews—to be infidels. Others blame Saudi Arabia's promotion of Wahhabism abroad for giving theological fuel to groups like Al Qaeda and the Islamic State, an accusation Saudi officials reject.

"Wahhabism is fundamental to the Islamic State's ideology," said Cole Bunzel, a scholar of Wahhabi history at Princeton University and the author of a recent paper on Saudi Arabia and the Islamic State. "It informs the character of their religion and is the most on-display feature, in my opinion, of their entire ideology." (May 31, 2016)

The Saudi double game—as both American allies and ISIS funders—clearly baffled the CIA, the State Department, and the White House. What American experts still have not grasped is that

ISIS clearly presented itself as the true guardians and rightful heirs of the Wahhabi tradition.

Scott Shane, of the *New York Times*, in his article entitled "Saudis and Extremism: Both Arsonists and the Firefighters," depicted the Saudi dual role brilliantly.

In the realm of extremist Islam, the Saudis are "both the arsonists and the firefighters," said William McCants, a Brookings Institution scholar. "They promote a very toxic form of Islam that draws sharp lines between a small number of true believers and everyone else, Muslim and non-Muslim," he said, providing ideological fodder for violent jihadists. Yet at the same time, "they're our partners in counterterrorism."

The reach of the Saudis has been stunning, touching nearly every country with a Muslim population, from the Gothenburg Mosque in Sweden to the King Faisal Mosque in Chad, from the King Fahad Mosque in Los Angeles to the Seoul Central Mosque in South Korea. Support has come from the Saudi government; the royal family; Saudi charities; and Saudi-sponsored organizations including the World Muslim League, the World Assembly of Muslim Youth and the International Islamic Relief Organization, providing the hardware of impressive edifices and the software of preaching and teaching. There is a broad consensus that the Saudi ideological juggernaut has disrupted local Islamic traditions in dozens of countries—the result of lavish spending on religious outreach for half a century, estimated in the tens of billions of dollars.

In 1964, when King Faisal ascended the throne, he embraced the obligation of spreading Islam. A modernizer in many respects, with close ties to the West, he nonetheless could not overhaul the Wahhabi doctrine that became the face of Saudi generosity in many countries. Over the next four decades, in non-Muslim-majority countries alone, Saudi Arabia would build 1,359 mosques, 210 Islamic centers, 202 colleges and 2,000 schools. Saudi money helped finance 16 American mosques; four in Canada; and others in London, Madrid, Brussels and Geneva, according to a report in an official Saudi weekly, Ain al-Yaqeen. *The total spending, including supplying or training imams and teachers, was "many billions" of Saudi riyals (at a rate of about four to a dollar), the report said.*

Hind Fraihi, a Moroccan Belgian journalist who went underground in the Brussels immigrant neighborhood of Molenbeek in 2005 and wrote a book about it, met Saudi-trained imams and found lots of extremist literature written in Saudi Arabia that encouraged "polarization, the sentiment of us against them, the glorification of jihad." The recent attackers, Ms. Fraihi said, were motivated by "lots of factors—economic frustration, racism, a generation that feels it." But Saudi teaching, she said, "is part of the cocktail" (August 25, 2016).

The fact remains that many private Saudi financiers and charities viewed the Islamic State as the rightful heir and offspring of Wahhabism, because it was as radical and sectarian as the original eighteenth-century Saudi–Wahhabi state. Meanwhile the Saudi regime—with their excuse of battling Assad and his Iranian military allies—refused to stop the flow of funds into ISIS or al-Qaeda in Syria. Or to its largest neighbor to the north, Erdoğan's Turkey.

"But, Uncle, what about Turkey?" Fioretta Novella asked. "It all seems very confusing over there!" She was right.

"President Erdoğan," I told her, "has played an incredible double game too. When the first riots broke out in Syria against Assad, he saw a chance to pose himself as 'defender of the Sunni.' Soon, Saudi money poured in from Riyadh so Erdoğan could play the central role of supporting these rebels to unseat Assad."

"So he helped ISIS?"

"And how! Erdoğan, with the Saudi and Qatari funding, empowered ISIS and the al-Qaeda group called Al-Nusra Front. Where did ISIS get all their weapons and supplies? And those white Toyota trucks? They were given to the Syrian Free Army rebels by the US State Department. But when they crossed the Turkish border into Syria, the Toyota trucks soon ended up in ISIS hands. The Turkish frontier with Syria is at least 500 miles long and foreign jihadis and their weapons have, for years, crossed freely. At the same time, Erdoğan's son has made millions of dollars, buying and selling ISIS oil."

"But, Uncle, if ISIS is threatening Europe with guns and bombs, how can Erdoğan help them? Isn't Turkey a NATO ally?"

"Of course, and they have the biggest army in NATO. But, he's playing a double-game. Three years ago, when ISIS appeared,

Erdoğan could have ordered his army across the border and ended it all in a few weeks."

"But why didn't he?"

I told Fioretta there was another plan—drawn up in secret by the Saudis, the Turks, and the Americans. It was a repeat of Afghanistan in the 1980s. Money flowed into Turkey from Riyadh while Erdoğan threw his support behind the Sunni rebels. Word went out for foreign jihadis volunteers, who crossed the Turkish border into Syria.

Obama first rejected the idea of trying to bring Assad to the negotiating table by arming the rebels. But then he changed his mind after intense lobbying by the Saudi king, the King of Jordan, and Prime Minister Benjamin Netanyahu of Israel. All argued that the US should take a role to try to end the conflict.

The CIA's covert program was the costliest in history—one billion dollars was spent in four years. Yet, it was an utter failure as exemplified by a Pentagon training program, launched in May 2015 and cancelled after only six months because it only trained sixty fighters the cost of nearly ten million dollars per trained fighter. Americans officially declared they were supporting "moderate rebels." However, many of those would in time cross over to al-Qaeda and ISIS.

It soon became a replay of the CIA's mujahideen program in Afghanistan that gave birth to al-Qaeda. In the Syrian conflict, CIA agents again repeated the same nightmare with Saudi-sponsored jihadi Wahhabi fighters. And then came the blowback. Saudi and CIA weapons ended up with Al-Nusra Front fighters. The iconic white Toyota trucks filled with triumphant ISIS soldiers were traced back to a US State Department gift to the Syrian rebels. In short time, they ended up in sleek convoys waving black ISIS flags in YouTube videos.

"And it was big business," I explained to my young niece. "Erdoğan adores his role of 'defender of the Sunni.' Don't forget, in the Near East, there is an old saying, 'the enemy of my enemy is my friend.' Erdoğan actually sees the Kurds as his greatest enemy. They're also Sunni Muslims, but with their own language and culture which is very different from the Turks. They always wanted their own homeland in an area that extends over parts of Turkey, Syria, Iraq, and Iran. Erdoğan deeply fears them."

"So, Erdoğan supported ISIS, so they would fight the Kurds?"

"Yes, he hoped ISIS would not only unseat Assad but also prevent Syrian Kurds from helping their Turkish Kurd brothers. But that game backfired once the Russians entered the war to save Assad and their only naval base in the Mediterranean. Erdoğan knew it was time to change his tactics so he could play a lead role in the future of Syria."

"So, you think ISIS days are numbered?" Fioretta asked.

"Yes, both big powers want to finish off ISIS. Now Turkey will position itself to profit where the wind is blowing, with both Russia and the US. Erdoğan's greatest obsession is the Kurds and he wants to prevent their foothold along his Syrian border. It is only a question of time before he attacks them."

"But what does Erdoğan want?"

"He dreams of a new Ottoman Empire in the Middle East. Who knows? Soon, he may even proclaim himself Caliph of Istanbul."

7

ORIGINS OF ISLAM

The greatest jihad is to battle your own soul, to fight the evil within yourself.

—PROPHET MUHAMMAD (PEACE BE UPON HIM)

FALL 2016

A few months passed. Fioretta approached me again with another question.

"So, if Wahhabism is not the 'true Islam,' can you tell me how Islam was born?" she queried.

"The faith manifests many different faces, but has one source." I answered.

Again we returned to *Arabia Deserta*, the historic name for Saudi Arabia. This landscape had always been parched and marginalized, a depressed cultural backwater in antiquity. Along the Red Sea coast stood a few ramshackle trading towns dotted with palms. In the scorched interior, Bedouin tribes fought, raided and squabbled over camels, possessions, and women. At night, tales were spun over campfires in the poetic tradition of their fathers and the fathers before them.

But in the year 610, the life of these Arabic-speaking desert nomads changed. In Mecca on a humid night, a pious forty-year-old merchant retreated to a cave outside the city to meditate. There, while in prayer, a ball of fire came to him. From this fiery vision he heard the word "Recite." Muhammad was stunned.

Then the voice spoke again: "Recite!" Muhammad's encounter with the archangel Gabriel was his first divine revelation.

Soon, jealous rumors threatened Muhammad, forcing him to flee Mecca with his small group of followers and take refuge in nearby Medina. This flight, known as *Hegira*, marked the first year of the Muslim calendar, 622. The literal meaning of the word for the new faith, *Islam*, is "submission," to the one and only God, Allah. Believers were called Muslims. Muhammad was viewed as the last prophet of the long biblical line that included Abraham, Moses, and Jesus. God's very words, revealed and transmitted to his chosen messenger, later gave birth to the holy Koran.

The Prophet died in 632 without appointing successor. Soon after, Islam was ripped apart by a central question. Who was his rightful heir? Who should become caliph, defender of faithful?

Muhammad had only one child, his beloved daughter, Fatimeh. She had married Ali, the Prophet's first follower, and gave Muhammad two grandchildren, Hassan and Hussein. For many Muslims, the Prophet's family were the clear heirs.

Yet power politics caused deep rifts in Islam. The patriarchs of the largest tribes bypassed Ali and chose their leader—the first caliph, Abu Bakr—through tribal consensus. These multitudes, their descendants, and converts would call themselves Sunnis, derived from *sunnah*, the tradition.

Those in opposition looked upon the Prophet's family as the only legitimate heirs, led by his son-in-law, Ali, and his grandchildren, Hassan and Hussein. This branch of Islam came to be known as Shia Ali, partisans of Ali. Because of his nonviolent nature, Ali accepted the first three community-appointed caliphs. But growing resentment exploded into a bloody uprising against the decadent third caliph, Uthman, in Damascus. Finally, Ali was chosen as the fourth caliph, but five years later he was assassinated. With his death, the corrupt son of Uthman proclaimed the Muslim world from Damascus, founding the Umayyad dynasty.

Since then, Ali's Shia followers have rejected all caliphs as usurpers. For this reason, the Arab Sunni, who now comprise 90 percent of the Muslim world, came to view the Shia as a dissident sect—revolutionaries to be persecuted and subjugated. Iran and southern Iraq remained Shia strongholds.

From the blazing sands of Arabia, Islam swept onto the high plateau of Iran only five years after the Prophet's death. Warriors under the fearful command of Omar, the second caliph, riding camels and flashing lances, appeared on the horizon. In 637, on the battlefield of al-Qadisya, the vaunted Sassanian imperial army of Persia was smashed. It was a humiliating finale to the glittering four-hundred-year dynasty that had humbled Rome. Almost overnight, twelve hundred years of Persian rule on the plateau came to a halt. In the patriotic epic of Ferdowsi, the invasion is lamented as "a national catastrophe." Henceforth, Iran became a subject nation of foreign conquerors, a piece of the Islamic mosaic that would stretch from stormy Atlantic breakers to frigid Himalayan snows to the South China Sea, along the archipelago called the Ring of Fire.

Omar's brutal conquest of Iran was followed by a migration of Muslims to the city of Kufa, now in southern Iraq, which soon became a refuge for Ali and his followers. Wandering Shia poets, merchants and other dissenters escaping Sunni persecution spilled into Iran, sowing Ali's teachings and the legitimacy of Muhammad's sacred bloodline. Ali came to occupy a special place in the hearts of Iranians. He preached social justice and respect for truth. His exemplary life is still a clarion call to faith.

Ali's son Hussein took as a bride the last Sassanian princess, the Shahbanou, who had been captured by Omar's troops. Their union symbolically tied the Prophet's family to Persia's royal lineage. Over the centuries, Shia opposition became the rallying point for the politically and socially discontented in the Muslim community. A revolt in 760 led by Abu Muslim, from the Iranian province of Khorassan, finally destroyed Umayyad power, giving birth to the glittering Abbassid caliphate in Baghdad, with its strong Persian–Sassanian influence. But another eight hundred years passed before the Shia faith was officially embraced by Iran's ruling elite. Today, Iran stands as the only Shia nation in the world.

As contentious as historic rivalry between the Catholic papacy and Luther's Protestants, the Sunni–Shia religious divide has fueled great bitterness over centuries. Standing at opposite poles, each still views the other the antagonist. Saudi Arabs will tell you that all Shias are heretics. While Shias condemn as illegitimate all caliphs after Ali, their faith is grounded in their belief in saints, called imams, who are all descendants of the Prophet. Ali and his two sons, Hassan and Hussein, are the first three imams.

Various Shia schools differ in the number of recognized saints: five among the Lebanese Druze, seven for the Ismailis, led by the Agha Khan. Iranians believe in twelve imams. The twelfth, Imam al-Zaman, or the Saint of All Time, mysteriously disappeared in the tenth century. He is the Shia messiah, or *madhi*, living in hiding, who will reemerge on judgment day to restore justice on earth. Throughout Iran, silent prayers are offered for his return.

Wahhabis consider this as sheer apostasy and their clerics have excommunicated Shia since Wahhab's day. Every Muslim who venerates their "saints" can be dispatched.

8

THE SHIA PASSION

Every day is Ashura, every place is Karbala.

—AYATOLLAH KHOMEINI

WINTER 2016

"Tell me more about the Shia," asked Fioretta. "How did they gain such a foothold in Iran?"

"It's simple. Shias are followers of Ali. Ali was Muhammad's son-in-law. He welcomed the newly conquered Iranians to Islam. In him they found their spokesman, their defender, their martyr, their saint," I explained. "As partisans of Ali, they could mourn their tragedies and pray for justice. Ali asked his Arab followers battling the Zoroastrians (the pre-Islamic religion of Iran), 'Have you read their holy book, *Avesta*? They have own faith and worship only one God just as we do.' Then his son Hussein married a Persian princess."

Imam Ali's wise words and nonviolent teachings were not loved by all. Some of his Arab brothers revolted against him, accusing him of being weak of spirit and loving foreigners. They killed him and then took the lives of both his sons, Hassan and Hussein. Hassan was buried in Medina in 670 in the famed al-Baqi cemetery—where his shrine would later be destroyed by Wahhabi hands. Ali and Hussein are both buried in southern Iraq, which explains why most of the country became Shia—followers of Ali. But to the east in Iran, the great conversion from Sunni to Shia Islam took place between the sixteenth and eighteenth centuries. Today, Iran remains the spiritual bastion of the Shias.

I described the Shia "passion play" (*taziyeh*) which is similar to the Passion of Christ. It begins each year in memory of the martyrdom of Hussein in the month of Muharram.

A lonely caravan travels east. Trudging across the desert of Arabia, noble Hussein, grandson of the Prophet, is on a holy mission. Citizens of the city of Kufa in southern Iraq have beseeched him to return and rule like his father Ali as the rightful heir to the Prophet. His caravan numbers seventy-two persons, including women and children.

The spiritual legacy of the Prophet is at stake. The new caliph, Yazid, is comfortably seated in opulent Damascus, new capital of the Islamic Empire. No one, not even the grandson of the Prophet, can stand in his way. Hussein knows that the caliph plans to kill him, but he does not turn back. He considers Yazid's rule unjust. Hussein's act of defiance is harrowing. He is prepared to die to save the purity of Islam.

Tragedy strikes on Ashura, the tenth day of the month of Muharram in the Islamic calender. The year is 680.

The caravan of Hussein will never reach Kufa. At Karbala, they face 10,000 warriors sent by the Caliph Yazid. Under the blazing sun, these soldiers mercilessly slaughter Hussein and his followers. This betrayal and butchery lies deep in the Shia psyche.

I described to Fioretta how the surviving women and children were taken to Damascus along with Hussein's severed head to be shown to the caliph. In a legendary scene of high drama, the great heroine of Islamic history, Zaynab—the sister of Hussein—was dragged into the caliph's court

"Who is this arrogant woman?" asked the angry Caliph.

Defiant Zaynab silenced him. "I will tell you, I am Muhammad's granddaughter. I am Fatimeh's daughter." Then she delivered a powerful, dramatic speech condemning the caliph for his atrocities against the family of the Prophet.

The courageous acts of Zaynab and her brother Hussein embody the nobility of the never-ending fight against tyranny and injustice, echoing the Jewish martyrs of Masada and the Passion of Christ.

The theater director Peter Brook described in a 1979 interview in *Parabola* magazine, the intensity and immediacy of the drama re-enacted each year, that he had once witnessed in the village of Neyshabur in northeastern Iran:

I saw in a remote Iranian village one of the strangest things I had ever seen: a group of four hundred villagers, the entire population of the place, sitting under a tree and passing from roars of laughter to outright sobbing—although they knew perfectly well the end of the story—as they saw Hussain in danger of being killed, and then fooling his enemies and then being martyred. And when he was martyred the theater form became a truth—there was no difference between past and present.

An event that was told as a remembered happening in history, thirteen hundred years ago, eventually became a reality that

moment. Nobody could draw the line between the different orders of reality. It was an incarnation: at that particular moment he was being martyred again in front of those villagers.

This defining moment of Ashura, the death of Hussein in Karbala, rivals the agony of Christ. But unlike the Christian ordeal, for the Shia there is no resurrection, no deliverance, only suffering and tears. Iranians will never forget or forgive Caliph Yazid for his crimes, or his general Shimr who killed Hussein and brought back his head. Yet the Sunnis do. This is why the divide between Shias and Sunnis is so irreversibly profound.

In stroke of genius, Ayatollah Khomeini tapped into the symbolism of *taziyeh*. As early as 1963, when rioting first rocked streets of Tehran, the future Supreme Leader broke with tradition and openly attacked the monarchy using the drama of Karbala. For years, Khomeini had branded Muhammad Reza none other than the ruthless Caliph Yazid. This illegitimate king embodied corruption and evil on earth. The suffering Iranian people had to rise against this injustice. Like Hussein, they had to prepare to fight for a noble cause. Yazid must go. The Shah must go.

And behind Yazid lurked, of course, evil incarnate: America, the Shah's longtime backer, perfectly cast in the role of the "Great Satan." Iran, Khomeini declared, had to be cleansed of plundering imperialists who acted with impunity, who took away God-given oil, who cultivated immoral pleasure and corrupted society.

In a nation scarred by centuries of foreign capitulation and humiliation, Khomeini's words struck a sensitive chord. Parliament had just passed a law forbidding courts to prosecute American military staff charged with a crime. In return, Iran was promised a massive infusion of US aid. Ayatollah Khomeini spoke out defiantly against this blanket diplomatic immunity: "Even if the Shah were to run over a dog belonging to an American, he would be prosecuted. But if an American cook runs over the Shah . . . no one will have the right to interfere with him. . . . I proclaim that this shameful vote of the Majlis is in contradiction to Islam and has no legality."

This criticism went too far. The government sent him into exile, first to Turkey, then to Iraq's holy Shia city of Najaf, shrine of Imam Ali, and finally to France. But Khomeini did not relent. His tape-recorded sermons were smuggled into Iran and heard in homes, buses, taxis and mosques across the country.

This was music to the ears of persecuted leftists, intellectuals, nationalists, Communists, students, traditionalists, and the clergy. All these opponents of the Shah found their rallying cry in Khomeini's uncompromising stance. United by their hatred for the "American-manipulated" Shah, the broad alliance needed a spark to light the fire.

The match was struck in January 1978 when a slanderous article denouncing Khomeini was published. Outraged theological students in the religious city of Qom marched in protest. Police responded by firing into the crowd. Several students died. According to the traditional mourning period, forty days later a procession was held for the fallen protesters. At the same time, in Tabriz, a similar procession took place and violence erupted. Again, the soldiers opened fire. More were killed, spawning mourning marches across major cities: Isfahan, Shiraz, Mashhad, and Tehran.

Over the summer, wildcat strikes in the oilfields and the bazaars and more processions brought temperatures to boiling point. Rising discontent sent thousands of demonstrators into the streets. By December, events reached a climax during the month of Muharram.

On December 2, 1978—the celebrated date of Ashura which falls on the tenth day of Muharram—two million people paraded in downtown Tehran, shutting down the city. The lead marchers wore red signaling their readiness to become martyrs. Many young women from the chic northern suburbs chose to wear the veil in protest. One month later, in January 1979, the Shah fled overseas and abandoned his supporters to their uncertain fate. This time no foreign-inspired coup could rescue his rule. Khomeini would return in triumph from Paris. The Karbela cycle was complete.

Yazid was gone.

The politicized *taziyeh* became a living theater. Mobilizing the ardor of the crowds, Khomeini and his revolutionary Komiteh committees turned on the wealthy Westernized Iranian elite, calling them idolaters, polluters, enemies of the people. Then he turned on his nationalist and leftist allies. When the dust finally settled over the land, his dream of an Islamic republic had become an unassailable reality.

On November 4, 1979, a few students penetrated the US embassy and seized their hostages. For a moment, the revolutionary leaders were hesitant about what to do next. But Khomeini understood the symbolic nature of their act. He saw the hostage taking, the Revolution, and "the Great Satan," all linked to the Karbala epic of Imam Hussein. In the two decades since 1979, the Islamic regime's moral role centered around the clergy's divine mission to purge the "Great Satan" and the "evil Yazid" from Iranian soil and soul.

In 1980, another event further fueled the Karbala paradigm. Lightning assaults, missile bombardments on the southwestern oil province of Khuzistan: Saddam Hussein's Iraqi armies invaded Iran by way of the Shatt-al-Arab. Imam Hussein's martyrdom was so potent in the Iranian psyche that Khomeini invoked it to rally the nation with his new battle cry: "Every day is Ashura, every land is Karbala."

The fighting reached a stalemate early on, but for the clergy, the war was a golden opportunity to capture the shrines of Karbala and Najaf in southern Iraq. The dream of liberating these hallowed pilgrimage sites where Ali and Hussein were martyred turned into a holy crusade. After centuries of grieving, it was time to punish the shameless Arabs and to avenge the historic crimes. Iraq was invaded.

Six years of unspeakable carnage followed, leaving more than one million dead and crippling Iran's petroleum centers of Abadan and Khorramshahr. The bitter stalemate ground on and on, like the horrific trench warfare of World War I. Volunteers charged across no man's land into a deadly haze of poison gas, minefields, barbed wire and raking machine-gun fire, often without any bullets to fire back. The cycle of martyrdom fueled hearts and filled the cemeteries. Fierce patriotism silenced all internal critics of the regime, and similar patriotism was also in Iraq. Streaming out from war-ravaged Khuzistan, millions of refugees trekked their way into slums and shantytowns, seeking safety in Shiraz, Isfahan, and Tehran. In Iraq, Baghdad and Bosra were flooded with refugees. Finally, after eight years of suffering, Ayatollah Khomeini announced in 1988 his greatest disappointment: "I drink the chalice of poison." With those words, the war ended.

Fifteen years would pass. Then, with the American invasion of Iraq in 2003, it all began anew. Again, the most sacred Shia sanctuaries found themselves encircled, at the center of an unfolding tragedy.

The bitter Saudi-Iranian rivalry played out dramatically in benighted Iraq, fueling sectarian politics and bloodshed that still curse Mesopotamia today. And, after yet another fifteen years, Iran remained still firmly under clerical rule, suppressing all public dissent with brutal crackdowns. Reformists and human rights activists languished in prison. Across the region, a dark cloak had fallen on the next generation as well.

HIDDEN FACES OF ISLAM: SUFISM AND THE POETS

O Marvel! A garden amidst the flames.
My heart has become capable of every form:
It is a pasture for gazelles and a monastary for Christian
*   monks,*
And a temple for idols and the pilgrim's Kaa'ba,
And the tablets of the Torah and the book of the Quran.
I follow the religion of Love: Whatever way Love's camels take,
That is my religion and my faith.

—Ibn Arabi

SPRING 2017

"And what about the Sufis?" Fioretta asked. "Who are they?"

"Ah, they are the mystics." I said. "Sufis belong to schools or orders formed around a Grand Master, their teacher. Many trace their lineage back to line of the Prophet and regard Muhammad as their spiritual guide. Sufis have a different vision, like Saint Francis. For them all creation is sacred: the animals, the wind, the rivers, the light. And all carry hidden messages for us, if we listen, if we see."

On a Sufi journey, the teacher is the guide. Parables, riddles and stories are told to gently enlighten the devotees. The goal is to dissolve the ego. Just as a Zen Buddhist monk seeks to empty the ego completely, a Sufi aims at emptying his inner vessel. On this path of mysticism, one empties the vessel can be filled with the bliss of divine love.

Huston Smith, an authority on the history of religions, wrote, "The Sufis are the mystics of Islam. Every upright Muslim expects to see God after but the Sufis are the impatient ones. They want God now, moment to moment, day by day, in this very life."

For a time, beginning in the twelfth century, Sufism was a mainstay of the social order for Islamic civilization, and since that time it has spread throughout the Muslim world. In fact, it was Sufi missionaries who spread first Islam into sub-Saharan Africa, Central Asia, and Indonesia. Still today the modern-day adherents cherish tolerance and pluralism, qualities that unsettle extremists, Wahhabis in particular.

Sufi schools are called *tariqah* and there are many—Naqshbandi, Nimatolllahi, Mevlevi, and countless others named after their revered founders. Devotees come to their gathering places where they sing, dance, pray, recite their rosaries in concert and listen to the discourses of their master, all to the end with reaching God directly. These practices have also produced some of the world's most beloved literature.

Sufi poets have captured this spirit over the ages. From Ibn Arabi of Seville, Al-Hallaj of Baghdad, Rumi of Konya, and Hafez of Shiraz, all these poets recited their love for the divine and their desire for mystic union.

Ibn Arabi describes: "When the mystery of the oneness of the soul and the Divine is revealed to you, you will understand that you are no other than God. . . . For when you know yourself, your sense of a limited identity vanishes, and you know that you and God are one and the same."

Sufi poetry also embodies a supremely tolerant vision of humanity and a decidedly non-judgemental philosophy of life, while being profoundly ecumenical. Take this poem "I Have Learned So Much" by the fourteenth-century poet Hafez, who syncretically fused his Koranic knowledge with the love poetry of earlier Sufi poets like Rumi and combined Zoroastrian symbology to create a liberating vision all his own.

> *I have learned so much from God*
> *That I no longer call myself*
> *A Christian, a Hindu, a Muslim,*
> *A Buddhist, a Jew.*
> *The Truth has shared so much of Itself with me*
> *That I can no longer call myself*
> *A man, a woman, an angel, or even pure soul.*
> *Love has befriended Hafez so completely*
> *It has turned to ash and freed me*
> *Of every concept and image*
> *my mind has ever known.*

Jorge Luis Borges, in his book *Seven Nights*, praised this fourteenth-century poet laureate from Shiraz. "I ought to have studied the Oriental languages: I have only glanced at them through translations.

But, I have felt the punch, the impact of their beauty. For example, that line by the poet Hafez: 'I fly, my dust will be what I am.' In this there is the whole doctrine of transmigration."

The Spanish poet Federico García Lorca also spoke of "the sublime amorous ghazals of Hafez." The German poet, Goethe, was so moved by the poet that he praised him higher than all others in literature. "Hafez has no peer," he wrote. Goethe then penned his *West–East Divan*, a collection of poems about Arabia and Persia, and even wrote essays on Islamic culture.

Ralph Waldo Emerson read Goethe's translation of Hafez in German whose mystical insights staggered him. The founder of American transcendentalism began to translate the master's poetry into English and wrote: "He fears nothing. He sees too far, he sees throughout; such is the only man I wish to see or be." And Emerson gave Hafez that grand and famous compliment, "Hafez is a poet for poets." Criticizing English poets—Wordsworth, Tennyson and Byron—he wrote: "It was no Oxonian, but Hafez who said, 'Let us be crowned with roses, and let us drink wine, and break up the tiresome old roof of heaven into new forms.'"

Even Walt Whitman, whose poetic voice heralded a new America, wrote in a style influenced by Islamic mystics. In his final days, he honored the debt in a poem entitled "The Persian Lesson." There is little doubt that Sufism influenced the American transcendentalist movement of Emerson and Whitman.

But, just as important, the Sufi vision also defiantly challenged the mullahs' strident dogmas. The act of drinking wine was frequently used as a metaphor by Hafez to describe his intoxication with divine:

What is the meaning of the water of life and
  the garden of Eram,
but delicious wine and the edge of this stream? . . .
The ascetic thirsts for the wine of Heaven's fountain,
Hafez wants his glass refilled. Whom will God prefer?

Always a positive humanist, Hafez never accused the weak; he excused them. He defended the downtrodden, reaching out to lift them up. For him, the flexible and imaginative character held the key to survival in troubled times. By staring at minute details, he insisted, one misses out on the grandiosity of God. Proclaiming himself a free spirit, he criticized the rigid morals of the clerics and their blind obsession of literally applying the letter of the law:

Do not judge us,
  Every man longs for the Friend, the drunkard as much as the
  awakened.
  Every place is the House of Love, the Synagogue as much as the
  Mosque.

He dismissed public postures of piety and despised religious hypocrisy. He openly challenged the clerics and even though he soundly condemned their rigid views, they never could banish his voice.

Today his verses are still sung by popular traditional musicians, heard in coffee shops over the radio, read at home, and transmitted from one generation to the next. His poetry resonates with such power and poignant meaning that every listener or reader takes it personally, as if it had been written just for him or her.

"When you hear his words, it's like he's speaking right now," my friend Akbar once told me, "This is what's so amazing. We turn to him," he continued, "whenever we feel lost, in pain, or of course in love. His poetry communicates with people of all levels. I can't really say why, but everyone, man or woman, has private conversations with him."

Many seek answers from the *Divan of Hafez*, his celebrated collection of mystic poetry, much as some of us consult our Astrology horoscopes. Even Queen Victoria was said to have consulted Hafez in times of need—which has been a custom in the Middle East for centuries.

The fourteenth century of Hafez was a chaotic and violent age. He watched as warriors on horseback threatened his beloved Shiraz time and again. But only rarely did any of this political turmoil seep into his poetry. Instead, his focus was fixed on his love of God.

When the Turkish conqueror Tamerlane (from today's Uzbekistan), loomed on the horizon, ready to sack the poet's city of Shiraz—having just annihilated every living soul in Isfahan and erected a tower with seventy thousand skulls—legend has it that he confronted Hafez face to face.

Hafez had written in a poem saying that he would gladly trade away both Tamerlane's royal capitals, Samarkand and Bokhara, for the affections a slender Turkish beauty. To the rash warrior-emperor, these words came as a grave insult against his native cities.

Hafez calmly offered this explanation: "Sir, because of my reckless extravagant excesses, you can see how poor I am."

Tamerlane's rage defused, and Shiraz was spared. Instead of being decapitated, the poet was rewarded.

Searching for the one poem that best captures the heart and humanism of the millions of Sufi followers worldwide, perhaps it would be these universal words written by Saadi Shirazi in his poem of "Children of Adam" that is often cited at the United Nations:

Children of Adam are all members of the same body.
Who, in creation, were made of the same essence.
If one part is wounded, the whole body suffers.
He who does not feel others pain.
Cannot call himself "a son of man."

10

THE SUNNI WORLD: PAST AND PRESENT

Egypt didn't change the basic tenets of Islam, but its cultural weight gave Islam a new voice, one it didn't have back in Arabia. Egypt embraced an Islam that was moderate, tolerant and non-extremist.

—Naguib Mahfouz,
Nobel Prize in Literature, 1998

SPRING 2017

"Uncle?" Fioretta asked. "I remember once you told me that Italy received gifts from the Middle East, down through the ages."

"That's right." I replied.

"Can you describe some for me?"

I began with some examples that she could find here in her own city.

"Here, in Florence," I said, "all you have to do is look at the aisle of cypresses in Boboli Gardens, or enter into Orsanmichele and gaze at the splendid mosaics of the tabernacle. But the best is the Brunelleschi's extraordinary *cupola*."

I explained how the first architect to design the project was not Brunelleschi, but Neri Fioravanti who had designed the Ponte

Vecchio. In 1367, Fioravanti envisioned a "double dome"—originally a Persian technique often used in constructing mosques. It was this technique that fifty years later Brunelleschi would design to build his famous dome.

"And it's no surprise that Florence and Isfahan are twin cities." I added.

"I want to know more!" she insisted.

"How many Italian family names have Arab roots—like Caracciolo, D'Alema, Galbani, Almirante?" I described the Emirate of Sicily that lasted 250 years, when Palermo was one of the richest ports in the Mediterranean. Many Sicilian names are rooted in that epoch. For instance, the city called Bagheria is linked to the Persian word for garden, *bagh*. Meanwhile, the word *qanat* describes the underground aqueduct systems of Palermo and Iran.

And then there is Spain's jewel of Cordoba once called "the ornament of the world" and legendary Alhambra of Granada. In fact, under Muslim rule, Andalusia was a luminary example of peaceful co-existence between Christians, Jews, and Muslims.

I explained that with the fall of Rome and the burning of the Library of Alexandria by Christian mobs, ancient knowledge was lost to the West for centuries. While Europe plunged into the Dark Ages, the new religion of Islam spread across the Middle East and North Africa to Sicily and then slipped across the Strait of Gibraltar into Spain.

When pillaging Crusades re-discovered the wealth and treasures of the East, they carried back to their villages: lemons, roses, cypresses, Egyptian gold, silks from Damascus, Persian carpets, orange seedlings, papyrus scrolls, precious stones. In their saddlebags were manuscripts with new knowledge of architecture, medicine, and algebra that was unknown in the West.

"Roses and cypresses and lemons?" she asked.

"Yes, and all the luxury trade—spices, pepper, silk, and gold—began flowing across the Mediterranean from the Levant's cities on swift galleys to Venice, Genova, Pisa, and Amalfi." This trade enriched the Italian city-states and sparked a revolution that would change all of Europe. Breakthroughs in science and math introduced Arabic numerals that quickly replaced the clunky Roman numerals. Imagine how much easier accounting became.

I told her that many scholars argue that the cultural bridges with the Islamic world saved the West. Greek texts and knowledge, lost to Europe since the collapse of Rome, soon flooded into Padua, Bologna, Florence, and Venice. The Classical world came alive again. This rebirth would change history by ending the Middle Ages and ushering in our modern epoch. It would be known as the Renaissance.

Days passed. We met again, and Fioretta came with more questions. Wars were raging in Syria, Yemen, and Iraq. She was still confused.

"But, Uncle, you told me that Iran is supporting the Shia in Iraq and also in Syria?"

"Yes, when ISIS threatened to overrun Damascus, the Iranians threw their full backing behind Assad, along with the Hezbollah and the Russians."

"So, then the Saudis are the great defenders of the Sunni?"

"No, they are not."

"But, the newspapers say—"

"A lot of journalists speak today about Saudi Arabia as if it was the heartland of Sunni Islam, but it isn't. Ironically, the great history of Sunni Islam has nothing to do with the Kingdom of Saudi Arabia."

To the point, I told her that Sunni Islam is over one thousand years older than Wahhabism. The word Sunni comes from the Arabic term *Ahlus Sunnah* which means "people of the *Sunnah*—the practices and verbal sayings of the Prophet."

Over the centuries, Sunni Islam evolved into four traditional Islamic schools of law. Today, Sunni followers count for more than 87 percent of Muslims and the schools are found in various regions of the world. The Maliki school is practiced mostly in North Africa; the Shafi'i school can be found along the East African coast and Indonesia; the Hanafi school lies in the heart of the Middle East—ranging from Egypt, Syria, Turkey, and Iraq to Central Asia; and the rigid Hanbali school is found only in the Gulf.

During a thousand years, Sunni Islam forged great imperial dynasties—the Umayyad, Abbasid, Mameluk, and Ottoman—that ruled from the eighth to the twentieth centuries across the culturally diverse Levant from wealthy cosmopolitan capitals of Damascus, Baghdad, Cairo, and Istanbul. The title of caliph finally rested with the Ottoman sultans, who welcomed the flood of Sephardic Jewish refugees from Spain in 1492 after their brutal treatment during the Spanish Inquisition. For centuries, both the Mughal Empire in India and the Ottoman Caliphate in the Middle East governed using the Hanafi school of law until the end of the caliphate in 1924. Throughout history, each dynasty expressed a tolerant face toward the multiplicity of cultures, faiths, and peoples that these empires ruled.

Today's Wahhabism has no claim or link to these great Sunni empires of the past. The Wahhabi doctrine—born only in the eighteenth century—never inched out of the Arabian Peninsula for its first two hundred years.

For over a millennium, Mecca had represented all the faces of Islam from Samarkand to Jakarta, from Dakar to Sarajevo. There were so many shrines in the city that some worshipers even took to calling it the center of the Sufi universe. The coastal strip on the Red Sea had always been a trading hub—an open, tolerant place where Yemeni, Levantine, and Egyptian merchants traded with pilgrims from distant lands. Few know that most of the populations of Jeddah, Mecca, and Medina in the nineteenth century were non-Arab Muslims—Bukharis, Javanese, Indians, Afghans and Central Asians—showing that these cities had always welcomed the larger world. Riyadh, was the opposite, rigidly closed in the burning heart of Central Arabia. Even now, the coastal Hejazis from Jeddah, Mecca, and Medina cling proudly to their unique memory as cosmopolitan traders and resent the heavy hand of the austere Riyadhis.

Today, Western journalists now speak only about the "Sunni–Shia" conflict. This suits the Saudis perfectly as they claim to represent the Sunni against their Iranian Shia rivals. Simply put, they prefer to call it an Islamic Civil War—from Syria to Yemen.

The Saudis see themselves under a region-wide attack by the Persians, in a Shia conspiracy to create pro-Iranian regimes in the shape of a crescent, across the Arab Middle East, stretching from Baghdad to Damascus and Beirut. And they consider the Shia minority in Saudi Arabia's Eastern Province as secretly loyal to Tehran, hoping to free themselves of the Wahhabi yoke when the time is right.

Armed with their army of lobbyists, the Saudi regime makes its case in Washington. To date, ten public relations firms are now on the payroll of the Saudi government, including the powerful and influential Podesta Group (the founder's brother, John Podesta, was the manager of Hillary Clinton's recent presidential campaign). *The Hill* recently estimated that Saudi Arabia spends over 1.3 million dollars a month for Washington lobbyists. Their hope is to line up the US government against Iran.

I ended our chat by telling Fioretta about a groundbreaking event that took place when Sunni leaders spoke out in unison against Wahhabism during an international conference in September 2016. Globally renowned Sunni scholars and clergy convened in Grozny, Chechnya. On the final day of this conference, all one hundred clerics unanimously took a stand against the *takfiri* Wahhabi terrorists who condemn and murder "non-believers," claiming to belong to the *Ahlus Sunnah* (the Arabic term for mainstream Sunni Muslims).

Egypt's Grand Imam of Al-Azhar, Ahmed el-Tayeb—the most prestigious figure in the Sunni world—with the unity of the clerics, declared that there are "dangerous deformations" of Sunni Islam that lead to extremism and terrorism and that a radical change was needed to re-establish the true meaning of Sunnism.

Their declaration clearly described the Sunni family. "The followers of the four (historic) schools—Hanbali, Shafi'i, Maliki, Hanafi—and followers of pure Sufism. Any other sects are *not* included in the Sunni community." Notably absent, were the Wahhabis and Salafis, dismissed as new innovations.

The Grand Imam Tayeb also spoke of "a return to the schools of great knowledge"—in Egypt, Tunisia, Morocco and Yemen, all outside of Saudi Arabia. These included Cairo's Al Azhar (the most important theological center of study in the Islamic world), Al Zaytuna University in Tunis, Tunisia, Al Karaouin University in Fes, Morocco, and the Hadhramaut schools of southern Yemen. No mention was made of the Islamic University of Medina in Saudi Arabia.

This was the first time that global Sunni Islamic scholars so clearly rejected Wahhabism as part of the larger Sunni family.

Then, Ahmad Karima, professor of Sharia Law at Al-Azhar University declared "If the world is looking forward to uprooting terrorism, it has to stand up against Wahhabisim because they are the root of all sedition and conflict."

Reaction to the Chechen conference was immediate and furious from Saudi Arabia. The imam of Riyadh's King Khaled Mosque, Adil Al-Kalbani warned: "The Chechen Conference should serve as a wake-up. The world is getting ready to burn us." The writer Muhammad al-Shaikh tweeted, "Tayeb's participation at the Grozny conference that dismissed Saudi Arabia from Sunnism will force us to change our behavior with Egypt. Our country is more important, and Sisi's Egypt shall go to hell."

After this gathering in Grozny, even more tectonic plates shifted on the eve of the Hajj. Iran's Supreme leader, Ayatollah Khameini launched an unusually harsh exchange with Saudi Arabia saying "The evil family tree of the Saudi dynasty does not have the competence to manage the holy shrines," referring to the 404 Iranians killed in the Mecca stampede the year before. He concluded that no Iranians would travel on the Hajj pilgrimage that year.

In response, the Grand Mufti of Saudi Arabia, Abdulaziz Al Sheikh, countered: "We have to understand that the Shia are not Muslims. . . . Their main enemies are the followers of Sunnah (Sunnis)." He then described the Iranian leaders as sons of *magus* or magicians, a reference to Zoroastrianism, the Persian pre-Islamic faith. His declaration cast a death sentence on the Iranian Shia. Fully aware of their Shia minority, the Saud royal family found themselves in a difficult spot. After this sectarian blast, the Grand Mufti was not allowed to deliver the Hajj sermon for the first time in thirty-five years. The House of Saud found themselves condemned by Sunni and Shia religious leadership alike—all in the week before Hajj. Their very "Islamic credentials" were at stake.

So, could the Saudis still call themselves "defenders of the Sunni faithful" after these leading religious authorities had verbally banished them from the Sunni world?

Well, a year later, the Saudis and Egyptian political leaders had reconciled, despite all the proclamations during the Chechnya conference by their own religious Imams. In six months, the Egyptian president Sisi was back under the Saudi wing. When the Saudis lashed out at Qatar, accusing their neighbor of supporting terrorism, many found the blaming finger-pointing disingenuous, as it was common knowledge that the Qataris had joined their Saudis brothers in financing the "Sunni rebels" that later mutated into ISIS and Al-Nusra Front.

Overnight, a quickly arranged boycott by Saudi Arabia, the UAE, and Egypt was launched. They pointed to Qatar's open relations with Iran, Al Jazeera's criticsm of the Saudi royal family, and ongoing support of the Egyptian Muslim Brotherhood. Due to the boycott, Qatar desperately turned to Turkey and Iran for military protection and food shipments. Ironically, Saudi Arabia and Qatar are the only two countries where Wahhabism is the state religion. But, Qatar had chosen not to follow their big brother. The backlash has begun in earnest.

I wondered about Fioretta's questions about the "Sunni–Shia" conflict. Perhaps it should be called the "Wahhabi–Shia" conflict. Or would it be more accurate to call it simply a "Saudi–Iranian Cold War."

Across the Middle East, this bitter rivalry had provoked untold suffering over decades. They distorted religion in a competition that fueled intolerance and sectarian violence. Extremists were mobilized. Women were forced to veil. Cosmopolitanism—once the hallmark of the Levant—was destroyed. Countless intellectuals were assassinated. This Saudi-Iranian Cold War for cultural supremacy was fought from the Nile to the Indus.

It had left lasting scars.

11
MESSAGE FOR THE YOUNG

I love you when you bow in your mosque, kneel in your
temple, pray in your church.
For you and I are sons of one religion, and it is the spirit.

—KAHLIL GIBRAN

"Now I'm beginning to understand why I rarely hear good things being spoken about Saudi Arabia." Fioretta sighed.

"Exactly," I replied. "Few fellow Muslims will offer kind words about Saudis. In my experience, most Northern Arabs—from Syria, Palestine, Lebanon, and Egypt—have always repeated the same refrain."

"But how is the country viewed?"

I then told Fioretta and her friends to do an experiment. "Why don't you approach any Muslim that you know and ask them how they feel about Saudi Arabia."

A week later, they came back to me describing anguished laments they had heard. One spoke about how the religion and holy shrines of Islam had been taken hostage, under Saudi control. Another recounted how the Saudis look down on other Arabs. Another spoke about how they flaunted their wealth in London and Geneva. Fioretta heard about alcohol being forbidden on Saudi soil and stories of drinking bouts in Paris, Beirut, and Manila, far beyond indiscreet eyes.

As the youngsters circled me, Fioretta asked, "But then, why don't Muslims protest or speak out against the Wahhabis?"

"How can they protest?" I replied. "Did you see what happened when the Abu Dhabi prince visited Florence? The mayor ordered all the Renaissance marble statues covered up just to please our guest. So, what can any ordinary Muslim do, if Prime Minister Renzi chooses to bend over like a supplicant servant?"

She was surprised.

I told her that most Arabs in Europe live with fear. They know that speaking openly or writing on social media is dangerous for them and their families. They risk repercussion and threats. In Italy, for example, Muslims know that if they speak out in public, within a day their relatives in Egypt, Tunisia, or Morocco will get a knock on the door by the secret police.

Then I asked Fioretta and her friends a question.

"Why do Washington, Paris, London, and Rome keep supporting the Saudi royal family and the Qatari monarchy?"

Their answer was a chorus of one word.

"Oil."

"Not only that," I added, "but they've invested billions in our economies. For example, in the United States alone, they've invested around 750 billion dollars. Every time that any criticism surfaces, they threaten to repatriate their immense fortune."

"And then, Uncle, what about the sale of weapons?"

"That is another shocking point."

I told them that today, Saudi Arabia is the world's second largest importer of arms with an annual budget of sixty billion dollars. Weapons manufacturers arrive in Riyadh from the United States, Canada, France, Great Britain, and also Italy. Saudi bombs that cascade on the fabled cities of Yemen are manufactured in Sardinia. And no captain of industry wants to sacrifice his shareholders' profit.

But, in the end, Wahhabism must be unmasked for what it is. And as the Sheikh of Al-Azhar in Cairo declared, it is not Sunni Islam. Quite simply, it is a small sect that originated in central Arabia only two hundred years ago. And yet, the havoc this doctrine has wreaked across the world is tragic.

For any young European or American, learning to pronounce the word Wahhabism will do more to clarify the chaos in the Middle East than any other. Refusing to allow Saudi Wahhabi funding for mosques or religious schools in Europe or America would be a constructive step forward. Indeed, each Islamic community can raise their own funds, as has always been the tradition in the past.

Each community requires a religious leader to lead the prayers. But this leader should also speak the national language, like Izzedin Elzir, the Palestinian imam of Florence—a leading figure of interfaith dialogue in Italy. Imam Elzir told me that he and his community had chosen not to accept one euro in funding from the Saudi foundation, the World Muslim League. He also went as far to say, "We're already encouraging imams to preach in Italian. If having this written down in a document is making non-Muslim Italians feel a bit safer, I don't see anything wrong with it."

In *The Guardian,* a recent review of *Islam: The Essentials* by noted scholar Tariq Ramadan states just how this change of mind is needed for western Muslims. Ramadan makes it clear that Islam is now a western religion, too—and he boils down his prescription to four L's: "Knowledge of the country's language, respect for its laws, loyalty to its society and liberty for the citizens."

Clearly, it is not in the interest of any community outside Saudi Arabia to import imams from Riyadh to spread the Saudi culture of oppressing women and pitting followers against their Christian, Jewish, Sufi or Shia brothers and sisters. Accepting Wahhabi mission funds only sows the seeds of what Brussels now suffers. Saudi-trained imams, by virtue of their doctrine, cannot embrace ecumenical dialogue, inclusivity, or integration until there are dramatic reforms to the texts and teaching in Saudi Arabia. It is time that civic and religious leaders in the West clearly understand this.

The European or American multi-cultural dream is built on integration, collaboration, and equal rights under citizenship. The Wahhabi mission rejects the very cornerstones of these principles. Until the Saudis allow free worship of all faiths in their country, the European Union and United States should respond in kind and curtail all imports of Saudi imams and their doctrine. Millions of Muslims—in Europe and America—will agree on this. They have witnessed years of moderate, traditional Islam being besieged and transformed by Wahhabi funding. We must help Muslims defend their culture and traditional faith against Saudi imperial ambitions. By speaking out, we offer solidarity, so they may also speak truth to power.

In the end, tolerance does not mean allowing destructive influences to thrive and threaten. As we know, fossil-burning fuels are fatally wounding our planet. Calling out the Saudi imperial projects is a responsible action we can take in this uncertain age.

Reciprocity is not a one-way street. It requires two partners, acting with understanding, speaking with grace and respect. It is time to realize that Wahhabism has been tearing apart the social fabric of the Middle East and the Islamic World. Their schools in France, Belgium, Kosovo and Bosnia are a threat to Europe. It is time to reflect, take a strong, clear position until Saudis decide to reform their society and, above all, their doctrine.

Young Fioretta and her friends did not make this world. They must live in it and thrive. Positive forces unite us; negative forces divide us. With their conscience and open eyes, they can choose enlightened paths to reach across the divide. By building bridges with empathy, they can shape their future.

A LETTER FROM THE AEGEAN SEA

I have the profoundest respect for people who behave in a generous way because of religion. But I come from a country where the misuse of religion has had catastrophic consequences. One must judge people not by what faith they proclaim, but by what they do.

—Amin Maalouf

SUMMER 2017

Dear Fioretta,

I write to you from the Greek island of Hydra in the sweltering heat with the good news that Mosul has finally been liberated from ISIS by Iraqi troops. Raqqa is about to fall to Kurdish forces.

But, as I told you, there is no cure for the ideology that has spawned ISIS. Wahhabism continues to spread across the world with Saudi financing. I witnessed this with my own eyes in Indonesia last March.

The noted historian/journalist Stephen Kinzer described in the *Boston Globe* the troubling events that recently unfolded in Jakarta.

Only a few months ago, the governor of Indonesia's largest city, Jakarta, seemed headed for easy reelection despite the fact that he is a Christian in a mostly Muslim country. Suddenly everything went violently wrong. Using the pretext of an offhand remark the governor made about the Koran, masses of enraged Muslims took to the streets to denounce him. In short order he lost the election, was arrested, charged with blasphemy, and sentenced to two years in prison. . . . This episode is especially alarming because Indonesia, the world's largest Muslim country, has long been one of its most tolerant. Indonesian Islam, like most faiths in that vast nation, is gentle, syncretic, and open-minded. The stunning fall of Jakarta's governor reflects the opposite: intolerance, sectarian hatred, and contempt for democracy. Fundamentalism is surging in Indonesia. This did not happen naturally.

Kinzer was right. A major factor came into play on March 1, 2017, when the Saudi King Salman landed in Jakarta with an entourage of over one thousand people—including princes, ministers, clerics and military—with 460 tons of equipment and luxury goods. The electoral campaign for Mayor of Jakarta was in full swing. His visit was part of a one-month Asian tour that began in Malaysia. In the Indonesian capital, the king—the Guardian of Mecca and Medina—was welcomed and celebrated with the highest honors.

Then, on March 4, the king descended from his private plane using his own personal gold staircase at the airport in Bali to begin an eight-day holiday with his whole retinue. They all settled in luxury hotels on the Nusa Dua Peninsula of the famed Hindu island east of Java.

During those days, your aunt and I went shopping for textiles on Sulawesi Street in Denpasar, Bali's capital. But this time, we noticed a big difference in the shops typically run by Muslim merchants. Remember? We had been there together two years ago over Christmas. Now, some shopkeepers were clothed from head to toe in black, with only the face showing. We had never seen this before. I greeted each with the Arabic words, "Peace be upon you."

"In which mosque do you pray?" I asked one lady.

She pointed, "The big one, down the street."

"Are there many Wahhabis now in Bali?"

"Oh yes," she replied with a big smile, "and we are growing everyday."

"Did you hear about the arrival of the royal family in Nusa Dua?"

"Of course," she replied. "They are very generous to us."

No sooner than King Salman had left Bali for Japan, massive demonstrations broke out in Jakarta. Enraged Muslim protestors flooded the streets, shouting against Basuki Tjahaja Purnama, known as Ahok—the standing governor of the capital.

Like Barak Obama in America, Ahok had made history. He was the first elected Christian Indonesian Chinese in a country with over 200 million Muslims—the largest Islamic population on earth. He enjoyed great popularity in his first term as governor with 75 percent of Jakarta residents satisfied or very satisfied with Ahok's performance as Governor.

He had bravely fought against corruption, cleaned up streets, reduced traffic jams, and earned widespread praise from long suffering citizens who marveled at their city's turnaround. His reputation reached to the far ends of the immense archipelago. Ahok was a sure bet to win re-election. But he made one fatal mistake.

On the campaign trail, one day, he told voters not to believe imams who quote a verse from the Koran to convince people not to vote for non-Muslim politicians, like himself. Meanwhile, Rizieq Shihab, notorious leader of the extremist Islamic Defender's Front (FPI) demanded Ahok be jailed for insulting Islam.

A final colossal rally took place in April. Buses poured in with fundamentalist enthusiasts from the countryside. This Islamist "tsunami" now enjoyed the full support of the ex-general Prabowo Subianto, who had been defeated in the prior presidential election. Indonesia's powerful military were still angry from having lost to civilians. Building up tension in the hard-line Muslim base was a key strategy of Prabowo's plan.

His ally, the Sunni organization FPI, had publicly incited violence against minorities and used hate speech to arouse mobs. Founded fifteen years earlier, the FPI began by attacking stores, bars, and nightclubs for selling alcohol or being open during Ramadan. The FPI members were widely known for hate crimes in the name of Islam and religious-related violence. This militia-like group of Muslim extremists was founded at the fall of Suharto's regime in 1998 and had been used before by the army and the police on several occasions. Now they stood out as power brokers in the election. The rest is history.

The shrill hysteria of the campaign scared Muslims across Jakarta and beyond. Ahok lost by four points. Then he was put on trial, convicted and locked up for two years in the company of murderers and rapists. It is evident now that Indonesia, long known for its tradition of moderation and tolerance, has entered a new dangerous phase. Wahhabi followers will be major actors in the political future.

Ibrahim, a friend of mine, sadly said, "When *Pancasila* goes, it will be the end." He was referring to the official foundation state philosophy that binds all Indonesians. *Pancasila* means "Five Principles." In this diverse amd multi-cultural vast nation, these principles unite the people across the sprawling archipelago:

1. Belief in one Supreme God
2. Just and civilized humanity
3. Unity of Indonesia
4. Democracy led by consensus
5. Social justice for all.

Now, the entire question of freedom of religion is at risk. The Saudi mission in Indonesia has been well crafted. At its heart is LIPIA, an Islamic university in Jakarta founded in 1980 and linked to Imam Muhammad ibn Saud Islamic University in Riyadh. LIPIA is tuition-free, with religious teachers from Saudi Arabia, and all instruction is in Arabic. Strict dress codes are enforced. Young men and women are separated. Music and television are forbidden. Even loud laughter is frowned upon.

Students study the ultra-conservative creed of Wahhabism. Meanwhile, Saudi financing has also constructed over 150 mosques across Indonesia as well as one hundred *pesantrens*, or boarding schools. Scholarships to Riyadh await the most promising pupils. When they return, they become the vanguard to spread Wahhabism across the Southeast Asian archipelago. LIPIA not only helps to shape a new Indonesian society, but it also provides the Saudis with a gateway to all of Southeast Asia. Their investments are paying off.

The Saudi imperial mission in Indonesia has been a long-term, patient and generously financed project to convert Indonesians to Wahhabi Islam. During his visit to Jakarta, King Salman announced that the quota for the Hajj has been raised. Now over two hundred thousand Indonesians can make the pilgrimage to Mecca each year—more than from any other country. Then, the Saudis asked the permission to open new branches of their LIPIA University.

In Muslim countries across Asia and Africa, similar efforts are being applied. Today, many in Washington and London consider it wasteful to spend money on "soft power" cultural projects that promote key values of tolerance, open society, and social justice. Yet, the Saudis view "soft power" differently because it works. Their well-targeted funds, charities, and missionary efforts are turning entire nations into hotbeds of fundamentalist Islam (notably Kosovo, Bosnia, Sudan, Pakistan, Afghanistan, the Maldives, Somalia, Chechnya, and now Indonesia).

The corrupt mismanagement of central governments in all these countries have spawned unemployed youth who are easily seduced by the promises of free food, a daily wage, and serving as religious warriors. The Saudis' dramatic success in reshaping Indonesia shows the importance of the global battle over ideas.

Across the straits in Malaysia, another special Saudi relationship has also borne fruit. The scandal-ridden President Najib Razak admitted that a 681 million-dollar gift was given to him by the Saudi king during his re-election campaign. This shocked most Malays, but President Najib Razak held on to power. Coinciding with the visit of the Saudi ruler, Razak announced the building of a new "center for peace" named after King Salman. Few Balinese can forget that Malaysia gave refuge to the *Jemaa Islamiyya* terrorist leaders before they plotted the 2002 Bali bombings.

Despite a reputation for religious tolerance, Malaysia is now the first Islamic country to outlaw Shias. The prominent Malay scholar, Asri Zainul Abidin, sums it up: "Malaysia is trying to become a country à la Taliban that only allows one school of thought." Across the Strait of Malacca, three million Shias in neighboring Indonesia are still able to practice freely for now.

In fact, in Central Java, there is still hope. Small grass-roots groups of Muslim women are emerging to peacefully and publically counter the Saudi influence in their culture. These women question why they should replace the richness of their own indigenous culture and dress with the Saudi colonial fashion import of black veil. There is a rising feeling that the Javanese identity is at stake and being overwhelmed by an Arab identity.

In Europe, populist politicians have provoked fear, calling for a backlash against Muslims. Marie Le Pen marketed her xenophobia and ignorance with crude racist emotions, as did Mr. Trump. Alas, they may not be capable of understanding the nuances of this reality.

Islam is not to be feared, nor to be blamed. Doors and windows need not be shut. Because of President Trump's controversial travel ban, the Iranian director, Asghar Farhadi, boycotted the Academy Awards even though an exception was made to allow him entry into the United States. On that night in Los Angeles, Farhadi won his second Oscar for the best foreign film, *The Salesman*. The first Iranian American astronaut, Anousheh Ansari, accepted the prize for him. Before the world, she read his statement.

> *I'm sorry I'm not with you tonight. My absence is out of respect for the people of my country and those of other six nations whom have been disrespected by the inhumane law that bans entry of immigrants to America. Dividing the world into "us" and "our enemies" categories creates fear. A deceitful justification for aggression and war.*
>
> *These wars prevent democracy and human rights in countries that have themselves been victims of aggression. Filmmakers can turn their cameras to capture shared human qualities and break stereotypes of various nationalities and religions. They create empathy between us and others. An empathy which we need today more than ever.*

On May 20, 2017, US President Donald Trump landed on his first overseas trip in Riyadh, the Wahhabi world capital. Fifty leaders of Muslim-majority countries had gathered for a regional summit focused on combating extremism. Trump spoke strongly against terrorism and its roots. "No discussion of stamping out this threat would be complete without mentioning the government that gives terrorists all three . . . safe harbor, financial backing, and the social standing needed for recruitment."

The American Lebanese journalist, Charles Glass, reporting on the event, provocatively asked: "Was he about to turn on his Saudi hosts and, as they say, speak truth to oil?" Of course, the answer was no. Trump was speaking about Iran.

Glass found it more than ironic that Trump avoided mentioning Saudi Arabia's historic role in promoting Islamist extremism. All Muslim leaders in the audience understood the roots of *takfir* (condemnation of heretics), but they remained silent. In the same report, Glass described the scene.

The sleight of hand went unremarked by his admiring audience. Everyone there knew who sponsors the Sunni Wahhabi Salafi extreme jihadists who have kidnapped and raped women in Iraq, Syria, and Nigeria; who have massacred Yazidis and Christians for being Yazidis and Christians; who have crucified, decapitated, drowned, and eviscerated those they deem opponents of their creed; who have beheaded Egyptian Christians in Libya; who have claimed "credit" for massacres against civilians in New York, London, Manchester, Brussels, Paris, Nice, Kabul and Baghdad; and who have sworn to destroy the Shia sect of Islam. It is not Iran. To the Salafi murderers, Iran is the Great Satan. No, Trump's audience knew well who sponsors the jihadis. As Walt Kelly's cartoon Pogo Possum said in 1970: "We have met the enemy, and he is us."

The journalist found Trump's hypocrisy galling.

Trump did not speak up for Saudi civil society activists in prisons, soon to be flogged or beheaded. He did not praise the Saudi women who risk arrest to force the princes to let them drive cars legally. He did not offer hope to the Palestinians under Israeli military occupation who demand the right of self-determination and an end to the absolute control of their lives that occupation entails. He ignored the democrats in the prisons of America's Middle East clients, whether Qatar, Bahrain, or Kuwait. Instead, he waved a flag for dissidents in one of only two countries in the region, the other being Syria, where the US has no leverage. He later commended Saudi Arabia, Egypt, the UAE, and Bahrain for imposing a boycott on Qatar, which supports a rival form of Wahhabi extremism and did not support a total interdict on Iran; the Arab states' demands include an insistence that the Qatari-funded media network, Al Jazeera, be closed down. Thus, he takes sides, not only in the Sunni–Shia divide, but within rival forms of Sunni Wahhabism.

King Abdullah of Jordan spoke after Trump and demanded that the Muslim leaders present condemn *takfiri* killers. He highlighted traditional, moderate Islam, and cited the Amman Message of 2006, when an historic consensus by international Muslim scholars agreed on:

1. Who is a Muslim;
2. Forbidding of *takfir*;
3. Recognizing the validity of the eight Madahib (Schools of Thought) of Islam. The theologians cited the four Sunni Schools (Hanafi, Sha'afi, Hanbali and Maliki), two Shia schools (Jaafar and Zaidi), and the Ibadi and Zahiri schools.

In raising the word *takfir* in the Riyadh conference, King Abdullah was surely pointing to the Wahhabi role in the ongoing tragedy in Syria. His country still shelters over 650,000 Syrian refugees.

King Salman of Saudi Arabia ended the meeting, agreeing with Trump, "The Iranian regime has been the spearhead of global terrorism since the Khomeini revolution." This statement caught many in the world by surprise.

Journalist Fareed Zakaria summed up Trump's embrace of the Saudis in his *Washington Post* opinion piece, "How Saudi Arabia played Donald Trump." He spelled out one glaring fact that the Saudis cannot conceal and I repeat it again here.

According to an analysis of the Global Terrorism Database by King's College London, more than 94 percent of deaths caused by Islamic terrorism since 2001 were perpetrated by ISIS, al-Qaeda, and other Sunni jihadists. Almost every terrorist attack in the West has had some connection to Saudi Arabia. Virtually none has been linked to Iran.

During his Riyadh visit, Mr. Trump announced with great fanfare and jubilation, a ten-year 350 billion-dollar arms deal with his Saudi allies. In the end, this military trade and the steady flow of oil have always allowed the Saudis to operate with worldwide impunity, free from public criticism, insuring blanket silence. After all, foreign arms deals keep the all-important Anglo American defense industries afloat. A member of British intelligence told me in confidence, "If British Aerospace doesn't sell our jets to Saudi Arabia, the French will, or even the Chinese. . . . Well, we simply can't have that."

Meanwhile, the Saudi bombings across neighboring Yemen continues. The entire country now faces widespread famine, according to UN agencies. To date, only muted criticism of the Saudi aggression has surfaced in the international press.

After the tragic collapse of the Arab Spring, Tunisia remains the only country still with a promise of democratic transition. Yet, like Indonesia, it too is under threat. Last month, a Tunisian woman who is a member of parliament and has spent seven years in government candidly told me in Rome, "We are investigating why so many young men went to Syria and Libya to fight for ISIS. We have heard countless accounts of how they were attracted and paid by recruiters financed by the UAE and Saudis. Poor, uneducated young men were offered a way to earn money for their family and promised insurance for the mothers in case they did not return." She then requested to remain anonymous.

In a closed-door session, this parliamentarian personally asked two diplomats from Saudi Arabia and the UAE why they were funding extremism in her country. The two diplomats pointedly told her, "We don't want democracy and Islam to meet. We don't want to hear any talk of human rights or women's rights. We don't want your Tunisian experiment of Islamic democracy to succeed."

So, my dear Fioretta, where do we go from here? From this Greek island of Hydra, I heard this morning the heart-breaking news of another massacre. Barcelona gripped the front pages. Since this book was first published last year in Florence, Italy, a terrifying pattern of carnage is being repeated across major European cities: from Barcelona to Manchester, from Nice to Berlin, from London to Brussels. What began on the night of November 13, 2015, with bombs and kalashnikovs in the streets of Paris has evolved into the new tactic of using hurling metal of vans or trucks as weapons to kill innocents. The profiles of the killers used to be ISIS foreign fighters returning from Syria. Today, they are young men who have radicalized through WhatsApp, Internet, or a local Wahhabi imam. In the case of the Barcelona attacks, investigators have already named an imam who may have inspired the young jihadis. And, yes, Abdelbaki Es Satty was a Salafi/Wahhabi imam.

One month ago, opposition politicians in London demanded release of a report commissioned by former Prime Minister David Cameron to investigate foreign funding of UK-based Islamic extremism and radicalization. The report looked carefully at the ideology and the financing flowing into Britain from abroad. Many believed that it cited Saudi complicity—allowing Islamic charities to fund and spread extremism in Britain. But, the current Prime Minister, Theresa May, made a shocking announcement and suppressed the report. She cited the need for "confidentiality." This begs the question, whose confidentiality?

In the House of Commons, MP Caroline Lucas accused Prime Minister May of burying the results of the investigation because publication would "embarrass the Government's friends in Saudi Arabia. Or is it because ministers care more about arms sales to Riyadh than they do about public safety in Britain?" Another opponent, Jeremy Corbyn, was also outraged: "If Theresa May is serious about cutting off financial and ideological support for terrorism, she should publish the suppressed report on foreign funding of UK-based extremism and have difficult conversations with Saudi Arabia, not hug Saudi and allied Gulf states even closer." How does such a democratically elected political leader feel that she does not need to answer such clear and urgent questions?

Yet again, the Anglo American establishment chose to favor Saudi military sales that fund their nation's defense industries, rather than speaking openly about the crisis at hand. Instead of protecting their citizens from future attacks, American and British leaders continued to treat the Saudi imperial mission with silence.

Raqqa may have fallen, but the chaos will continue.

And so, Fioretta, I leave you with these last words. You asked me months ago to help you understand what is happening in today's Middle East. As you've discovered, there is a distinct reason for your confusion. The truth has yet to be revealed to the broader public. In fact, it has been censored by powers at the highest level. And as you fall asleep this evening, it still remains—the best-kept secret.

THE ROAD TO SAMARKAND

*Samarkand is the beauty of the earth, but Bukhara is the
beauty of the spirit, and in all other parts of the globe, light
descends upon the earth.*
From holy Bukhara it ascends.

—UZBEK SAYING

WINTER 2017

Summer winds cooled. Seasons turned. On a brisk autumn evening, we surprised Fioretta with an offer to travel to her first
Muslim country. She had only faintly heard of Samarkand and
Bukhara. Our friend and Medieval scholar, Franco Cardini, was
leading a group to Uzbekistan and we decided to join him; it was
now or never. She was visibly excited; our journey would fall during
her November break. After much pleading, her father agreed.

Before leaving, I told her that now *Saudimania* was in the air.
The "Man who would be King"—thirty-two-year-old Crown
Prince Mohammed bin Salman, commonly known as MBS, who
was appointed by his father in June—would soon inherit his father's
throne. Hailed as a reformer by the press, he was also viewed as an
impulsive, even reckless, hothead. The Saudis' great fear that they

would be openly blamed sooner or later for decades of jihadist violence seemed to fade with Trump's hearty embrace during his official visit to Riyadh.

Now, American PR companies were hard at work to change the country's image. MBS was being presented as the driving force behind Saudi Arabia's attempt to diversify its economy. Lofty plans were unveiled of a 500 billion-dollar high-tech mega-city called Neom. Thirty-three times the size of New York, it bordered Jordan and included a sharia-free new tourist resort on the Red Sea. Then MBS announced he would lift the ban on women driving and "restore a moderate, tolerant Islam" to Saudi society. Audacious words. The word "restore" was misleading because since the birth of Saudi Arabia in 1930, "tolerance" had never existed.

The *New York Times* journalist Thomas Friedman flew to Riyadh and interviewed the young prince. In his gushing op-ed, Friedman whitewashed thirty years of Saudi financing of Wahhabi jihadists. "After nearly four hours together, I surrendered at 1:15 a.m. to [MBS's] youth, pointing out that I was exactly twice his age. It's been a long, long time, though, since any Arab leader wore me out with a fire hose of new ideas about transforming his country."

He got a quick rebuke from Thomas Erdbrink, the *New York Times* bureau chief in Tehran, who tweeted, "*BREAKING:* Saudi Arabia, which has funded extremist Wahhabi mosques across Europe, to become beacon of liberal Islam!"

And another from foreign affairs journalist Avi Asher-Schapiro who tweeted, "Over multiple courses of lamb in Riyadh, the Saudi

Crown Prince easily convinced Tom Friedman that he's a genuine reformer, mega-popular dude, and an all around super awesome guy."

Charles Glass added a wry note: "It's like John Gotti leading the War on Crime."

Nonetheless, Friedman's high-visibility *New York Times* profile was a coup for Saudi Arabia's PR machine hard at work to change the country's image. In almost two years, from 2015 until 2017, the Saudi government had spent eighteen million dollars in Washington on lobbyists—with 145 well-connected ex-senators, congressmen, and retired ambassadors on the Saudi payroll. In harmony, this PR chorus took their cue from Riyadh and began chanting about the newly found freedoms of Saudi women.

It was then that I read about the ongoing campaign to end the law of "male guardians" who control the life of every Saudi woman. This discriminatory law exists nowhere else on earth, a Saudi woman activist friend told me. "Until this law is removed," she said, "we remain skeptical of any government statement concerning our rights." The Saudi women's movement carries the appropriate slogan: "I am my own Guardian."

The new Saudi public image that had its debut with the theatrical visit of Trump on May 20, 2017 rose to operatic heights on November 4 with the dramatic televised resignation of the Lebanese Prime Minister Hariri in Riyadh. This act was then followed by a sweeping crescendo of anti-corruption arrests across the kingdom that rounded up over two hundred family members and business elites and bundled them all into the posh Ritz Carlton, the world's first five-star prison.

The tactic was clear—the corruption charges silenced any public opposition while collecting badly needed revenue. Six months before, when King Salman proclaimed his son heir to the throne, he broke the succession tradition in the Saud family by which the throne passed to a brother or cousin of the king. Instead, King Salman elevated his own son, provoking internal conflict. A dynasty was in the making. For the crown prince—still Minister of Defense—this moment was all about consolidating power. *Game of Thrones* in the Arabian Desert.

Rumors abounded. Would the crown prince really cut off funding of the "Wahhabi Mission" and the World Muslim League that channeled Wahhabism across the globe? Or would he continue to play the Saudi "double game" with the West? Could he truly force the imams to modify the teachings of Abdul Wahhab or would that spark an ultra-conservative backlash, like the siege of Mecca in 1979?

Then, France 24 flashed the headline: "Saudi Arabia's anti-corruption prince buys $300 million French chateau." The Chateau Louis XIV, near Versailles, broke the record as the world's most expensive residence. The crown prince's purchase was extravagant, even for Saudi royals. But that was not all. A year earlier on the French Riviera, MBS impulsively bought a 440-foot yacht from a Russian tycoon for 500 million dollars. While MBS preached austerity at home, he spent lavishly abroad.

Meanwhile, the young crown prince, in his role as Minister of Defense, had brashly lashed out at a host of foreign rivals. However, most of these actions had backfired—the failed blockade of Qatar, the calamitous war in Yemen, the embarrassing "resignation" of Lebanese Prime Minister Hariri, and the defeat of Saudi-backed rebels in Syria with the collapse of ISIS.

The embargo against Qatar began in June 2017, just after Trump departed from Riyadh. Doha stood accused of financing terrorism. In truth, this was an attempt to end the Qatari Emir's independent foreign policy—that supported the Muslim Brotherhood, while also having ties with Iran (with whom Qatar shares an immense offshore gas field in the Persian Gulf). All this smacked of great hypocrisy.

Meanwhile, MBS's war in Yemen failed to provoke regime change. The Shia Houthi rebels—seen as supported by Iran—still controlled the capital Sana'a. The Saudi military campaign, estimated to have cost 100 billion dollars, had created a devastating tragedy on the ground. Air strikes, bombings, and blockading of ports had brought only hunger and death. The UN called it "the world's worst humanitarian crisis." Over eight million people faced starvation and over one million suffered from a cholera epidemic.

In Beirut, Prime Minister Hariri returned from Riyadh after his forced resignation and was welcomed home like a hero. MBS's attempt to dissolve parliament and remove the Iranian-backed Shia party Hezbollah from power had provoked an opposite reaction. The country's disparate factions rallied together behind Hariri. He promptly reassumed power.

Saudis, still lamenting the failure of their intervention in Syria, nervously read reports that found their fingerprints and those of their CIA partners on weapons of ISIS. One recent report by *Conflict Armament Research*—an organization that tracks arm shipments—examined forty thousand recovered arms: it states that weapons supplied to Syrian rebels by the CIA and Saudi Arabia often ended up in ISIS hands. One shocking case pointed out how only two months after leaving the factory, anti-tank weapons the CIA secretly transferred to Syrian rebels ended in the hands of ISIS.

Across the region, it seemed that MBS's grand campaign against Iranian influence in Qatar, Yemen, Lebanon and Syria was failing.

Yet, he had begun repeating the Israeli Prime Minister's words— referring to Iran as Saudi Arabia's "existential threat." For years, Prime Minister Netanyahu, with his PR spin on the world stage, had successfully used Iran to deflect from Israel's ongoing occupa- tion of Palestine. Now, the crown prince was using the same words to deflect any criticisms of his internal reforms and Saudi's dark past with ISIS and al-Qaeda. For his Wahhabi subjects, the crown prince's public loathing of Iran reinforced the view that, across the Arab world, the Shia could be labeled as "Iranian agents," unbeliev- ers deserving punishment. MBS had ensured that the Wahhabi hatred of the Shia was officially left intact.

Israel and MBS now share a mutual enemy—Iran—and this has brought them together, and the American president could not be happier. I wondered whether Trump's son-in-law, Jared Kushner— Bibi Netanyahu's family friend of many years—had promised the crown prince unyielding American military support in return for his Saudi–Israeli alliance, as well as his massive purchases of Amer- ican weapons, and his targeting of Iran.

Adding fuel to the fire, Trump declared America's recognition of Jerusalem as Israel's capital. Overnight, the dormant Palestinian cause was re-ignited. During seven years of the Arab Spring, the press coverage of the Israel–Palestine conflict had been completely overshadowed by ISIS and the Syrian civil war. But with one stroke, Trump put it back on the front burner, attracting global condemnation at the United Nations General Assembly.

Before leaving Florence, I sat Fioretta down.

"Actually," I explained, "there is one Muslim country that has rejected Wahhabism completely. This is where we are going—Uzbekistan." And when Idanna and I boarded the plane in Rome bound for Tashkent on the Silk Road in the heart of Central Asia, Fioretta was with us.

At the crossroads of China, Russia, India, and Iran, this land was once a glowing beacon for the Islamic world. Together with our young niece, we walked down backstreets and into squares of the two fabled oasis-cities of Bukhara and Samarkand, long revered as centers of illuminated learning, rivaling Cordoba, Damascus, Cairo, Isfahan, and Baghdad.

We found ourselves in a nation forging its new identity by reaching back into the ancient past, after shrugging off seventy years of drab-gray Soviet domination.

Flanked to the east by the lofty Pamir Mountains, Samarkand sits in the fertile valley of the Zerafshan River, the famed imperial capital of the world-conqueror Tamerlane. Known over the centuries as the *Center of the Universe, Garden of the Soul, Jewel of Islam,* and *Pearl of the East,* this remote city of legends lost in the Asian continent has attracted travelers over the centuries like an exotic talisman. They arrived full of wonder.

The classic poem "The Golden Road to Samarkand" by the English poet James Flecker, who served in the consular service in the Eastern Mediterranean, spelled out city's magnetic pull in 1913. "For lust of knowing what should not be known, we make the golden journey to Samarkand." Difficult to reach, it had always been a mythic destination with its turquoise domes and mosque facades adorned with the spellbinding geometry of sky-blue tiles, multi-colored majolica and Koranic verse.

To the south lay Bukhara, the city protected by an eight-mile wall, and once known as "the noble, the sublime" also because of its people considered the most civilized in Central Asia. In the tenth century, its rich bazaars teemed with Iranians, Jews, Indians, Afghans, Tartars, and Chinese trading silks, jewelry, spices, and jade going west, while amber, furs, silver, and horses heading east.

The writer Colin Thubron, who tromped across Asia from China to Turkey in his *Shadow of the Silk Road*, described that epoch.

It was an ebullient age. Persian music, painting, and wine flourished heretically alongside Koranic learning, and the great library of Bukhara, stacked with 45,000 manuscripts, became the haunt of doctors, mathematicians, astronomers, and geographers. This epoch fostered universities that produced such geniuses as al-Biruni (who first computed the radius of the earth); the lyric poet Rudaki; and the great Ibn Sina, known in the West as Avicenna, who wrote 242 books of stupefying variety, and whose Canons of Medicine *became a vital textbook in the hospitals of Christian Europe for over 500 years.*

In 1498, four centuries later, the grandson of Tamerlane, Ulugh Beg, built his state-of-the-art observatory in Samarkand to study the night sky. He then mapped out a celestial atlas citing 1,022 stars by using his extraordinary invention, the largest sextant ever constructed. Considered one of the great astronomers of all time, Ulugh Beg wrote: "Religion disperses like a fog, kingdoms perish, but the works of scholars remain for an eternity."

He was prophetic. Sovereigns and empires rose and fell before the Bolsheviks entered the valley and shelled Samarkand with artillery. But the scientific discoveries of Ulugh Beg inspired not only Galileo but generations of star gazers thereafter.

After the collapse of the Soviet Union, independent Uzbekistan tried to shape a new identity. And what better way than to re-connect with the Islamic past? But at that moment, something pivotal happened.

Saudi funding started to pour in with foreign imams who set up madrasas to convert the Uzbek people to the Wahhabi doctrine. A few years passed. Then, armed conflict broke out between jihadis and government forces—first in the Ferghana Valley and then, in 1999, five bombs exploded in the capital Tashkent. A sixth almost took President Islam Karimov's life.

The government quickly accused the IMU—the Islamic Movement of Uzbekistan—and outlawed anyone who was proselytizing. In a heartbeat, the Wahhabi mission was terminated and their imams sent home. Meanwhile, many IMU fighters found refuge in the mountains of Afghanistan and in Pakistan, where they remain today.

Uzbekistan turned back to its own cultural roots. Tamerlane, the empire builder, was trumpeted as the national hero. His towering statue dominated a large central square in Samarkand.

With Fioretta, we drove twelve kilometers outside Bukhara to Qasr-i-Arifan, the birthplace of Naqshband, the country's most famous Sufi saint. With him, the richest mystical tradition of Central Asia was born, by far the most widespread Islamic practice in Uzbekistan. The great mystic had died in that village and his tomb was a centuries-old site brimming with spirituality, surrounded by a verdant garden exuding great tranquility. The order founded by Sheikh Bahauddin Naqshband today is one of the largest Sufi orders in the world with millions of followers.

At the tomb of the saint, pilgrims came and went. Everyone whispered a prayer and left an offering. Everyone caressed the white marble. Some chanted quietly, the same words in repetition, a practice of Naqshbandi followers. In the middle of the garden, a huge fallen elm tree, planted by the saint five centuries earlier, lay in state horizontally. Protected by a wooden fence, it had become a relic venerated like the tomb. The hands of the pilgrims touched the wood, now fossilized, but forever inhabited by the spirit of the saint. Stripes of colored fabrics left as prayers waved from the branches in the breeze. The women wore colorful clothes and walked freely among the fountains in the well-tended garden. No woman was dressed in mourning or with her head covered in black.

These Uzbeks understood well that the Wahhabis would have destroyed their sanctuaries, erasing all traces of the mystic Naqshband, labeling all of them *kafirs* or heretics.

We watched the smiles of these pilgrims as they connected with their holy teacher. Traditional Islam had won its struggle against the grave Saudi threat.

Back in Samarkand, we stumbled across a wedding party that swept towards us, the newlyweds in the midst of a crowd of well-wishers advanced dancing to the sound of traditional music blaring out of a huge boombox. Fioretta smiled, moving to the beat. The message was clear. In the cultural past lay the future.

The proud groom swayed with his beaming bride in her white dress that highlighted her beauty. Then, the couple stopped to pose for a photographer. In the background soared the immense façade of the great Tilya-Kori mosque and Koranic school on the majestic Registan Square.

"Pity that Saudi women cannot live their Islam as the women do here in Samarkand!" Fioretta said in a low voice as if speaking to herself.

Notes

PROLOGUE

2 **The analysis of the Global Terrorism Database:** Fareed Zakaria, "How Saudi Arabia Played Donald Trump," *Washington Post*, May 25, 2017; https://www.washingtonpost.com/opinions/global -opinions/saudi-arabia-just-played-donald-trump/2017/05/25 /d0932702-4184-11e7-8c25-44d09ff5a4a8_story.html.

4 **According to the *Financial Times*:** Simon Kerr, "Saudi Arabia to Launch Global PR Offensive to Counter Negative Press," *Financial Times*, September 12, 2017; https://www.ft.com/content/c7d57f8e -96ca-11e7-a652-cde3f882dd7b.

7 **Fifteen minutes later, on the set, she began:** Christiane Amanpour, "Author on the Link between Wahhabism and Jihad," CNN, interview, December 21, 2018; https://edition.cnn.com/videos/tv /2018/12/21/amanpour-terence-ward-the-wahhabi-code-how -the-saudis-spread-extremism-globally.cnn.

9 **The article explained "How MBS Hit a Dead End":** Bobby Ghosh, "How Mohammad Bin Salman Hit a Dead End in Washington," Bloomberg, May 4, 2020); https://www. bloombergquint.com/gadfly/saudi-arabia-s-crown-prince -mbs-is-right-where-trump-wants-him.

10 **Fareed Zakaria described the export of Wahhabism:** Fareed Zakaria, "Saudi Arabia: The Devil We Know," *Washington Post*, April 21, 2016; https://www.washingtonpost.com/opinions /saudi-arabia-the-devil-we-know/2016/04/21/2109ecf6-07fd -11e6-b283-e79d81c63c1b_story.html.

11 **Abdullah al-Alaoudh challenged:** Abdullah Alaoudh, "MBS Is Not Saudi Arabia," interview with Saudi scholar, Al-Jazeera TV, June 28, 2019; https://www.aljazeera.com/programmes /talktojazeera/2019/06/saudi-scholar-alaoudh-mbs-saudi -arabia-190626131438417.html.

12 **Violence against Shia communities:** Terence Ward, "The Chilling Message of the Saudi Executions," CNN, May 9, 2019; https://edition.cnn.com/2019/05/08/opinions/saudi-arabia -shia-executions-message-ward/index.html.

14 **Ben Hubbard confirmed MBS fears:** Ben Hubbard, *MBS: The Rise to Power of Mohammed bin Salman* (New York: Tim Duggan Books, 2020).

15 **Decades of funding by Saudi Arabia's World Muslim League:** Krithika Varagur, "How Saudi Arabia's Religious Project Transformed Indonesia" *The Guardian*, April 16, 2020; https://www .theguardian.com/news/2020/apr/16/how-saudi-arabia -religious-project-transformed-indonesia-islam?CMP=Share _AndroidApp_Gmail.

16 **Saudi clerics are considering destroying:** "Saudi Regime Hell-bent on Wiping Muslim Heritage in Hejaz," *Islam Times*,

August 30, 2019; https://www.islamtimes.org/en/news/813551
/saudi-regime-hell-bent-on-wiping-muslim-heritage-in-hejaz.

18 **Madawi al-Rasheed, recently offered:** Madawi al-Rasheed,
"The Saudi Lie," talk in Griffith University, Conservatorium
Theatre, South Brisbane, Queensland, Australia, October 26
2019; https://www.youtube.com/watch?v=BoDsE5Uh08E.

19 **Lebanese author Kim Ghattas:** Kim Ghattas, *Black Wave:*
Saudi Arabia, Iran, and the Forty-Year Rivalry That Unraveled
Culture, Religion and the Collective Memory in the Middle East,
New York: Henry Holt, 2020.

CHAPTER 1

27 **The fourth imperial project:** Kamel Daoud, "Saudi Arabia,
an ISIS That Has Made It." *New York Times,* Nov. 20, 2015,
https://www.nytimes.com/2015/11/21/opinion/saudi-arabia-an
-isis-that-has-made-it.html.

29 **The element that all five imperial projects share:** A host of
articles support the ideology of Wahhabism serving as a key
inspirational source for Euro-jihadists, ISIS, al-Qaeda, Boko
Haram and even the original Taliban who were students in
Wahhabi-funded madrasas in Quetta, Pakistan, including:

> Fareed Zakaria, "Saudi Arabia, the Devil We Know,"
> *Washington Post*, April 21, 2016.
> David Kirkpatrick, "ISIS' Harsh Brand of Islam Is Rooted in
> Austere Saudi Creed," *New York Times*, September 24, 2014.

Robert Fisk, "Saudi Arabia: the history of hypocrisy that we chose to ignore," *The Independent,* January 14, 2015.

Bernard Haykel, "On the Nature of Salafi Thought and Action," in *Global Salafism: Islam's New Religious Movement,* ed. Roel Meijer. Hurst: London, 2009.

Scott Shane, "Saudis and Extremism: Both Arsonists and the Firefighters," *New York Times,* August 25, 2016.

32 **Congressional testimony:** US Dept of Treasury, Testimony of Stuart Levey, Under Secretary Office of Terrorism and Financial Intelligence U.S. Department of the Treasury Before the Senate Committee on Banking, Housing, and Urban Affairs July 13, 2005. https://www.treasury.gov/press-center/press-releases/Pages/js2629.aspx.

CHAPTER 2

38 **Wahhabism is definitely an intolerant form of Islam:** Bernard Haykel, Madawi al-Rashid, Aimen Dean, Matthew Levitt, and Mohammed Yahya, "Is Saudi Arabia to blame for the Islamic State?" BBC, December 19, 2015, http://www.bbc.com/news/world-middle-east-35101612.

39 **"ISIS Theology Directly Linked to Wahhabism":** Bernard Haykel, Madawi al-Rashid, Aimen Dean, Matthew Levitt, and Mohammed Yahya, "Is Saudi Arabia to blame for the Islamic State?" BBC, December 19, 2015, http://www.bbc.com/news/world-middle-east-35101612.

CHAPTER 3

49 **charged as the first defendant by the International Criminal Court:** Gabriele Steinhauser, "Islamist Sentenced to Nine Years for Timbuktu Shrine Destruction," *Wall Street Journal,* September 27, 2016.

50 **Sheikh Adil al-Kalban:** "Leading Saudi Cleric: Daesh ISIS have the Same Beliefs as we do," MBC DUBAI, January 22, 2016. https://www.youtube.com/watch?v=GWORE6Obfhc.

CHAPTER 4

56 **Few Westerners know:** Cole Bunzel, *The Kingdom and the Caliphate: Duel of the Islamic States,* Carnegie Endowment for Peace: New York, 2016.

56 **Uthman ibn Bishr:** Also known as Uthman ibn 'Abd Allah ibn Bishr, he recorded the history of the Najd in what would come to be known as the Wahhabi Manuscript:

> Uthman ibn Bishr, *Unwan al-majd fi ikipe Najd* [The mark of glory in the history of Najd], ed. Abd al-Rahman ibn Abd al-Latif Al al-Shaykh, Riyadh: Darat al-Malik Abd al-Aziz, 1982, 1: 257–258.

CHAPTER 5

63 **Juhayman Al-Otaybi:** Juhayman ibn Muhammad ibn Sayf al-Otaybi (9/16/1936–1/9/1980) was a Saudi religious extremist and former Saudi Arabian army man who in 1979 led the Grand

Mosque seizure of the Masjid al Haram in Mecca, to protest against the Saudi monarchy.

Daniel Lazare, "How U.S.–Saudi Marriage Gave Birth to Jihad," *The American Conservative*, November 2, 2017, http://www.theamericanconservative.com/articles/how-us-saudi-marriage-gave-birth-to-jihad/.

66 **Ziauddin Sardar:** Born in Pakistan on 10/31/1951, he is a London-based scholar, award-winning writer, cultural critic and public intellectual who specializes in Muslim thought, the future of Islam and cultural relations.

Ziauddin Sardar, "The Destruction of Mecca" *New York Times,* September 30, 2014, https://www.nytimes.com/2014/10/01/opinion/the-destruction-of-mecca.html.

68 **"This is the end of history in Mecca and Medina and the end of their future":** Raya Jalabi, "After the Hajj: Mecca Residents Grow Hostile to Changes in the Holy City," *The Guardian*, September 14, 2016, https://www.theguardian.com/cities/2016/sep/14/mecca-hajj-pilgrims-tourism.

68 **Sheikh ibn Baz, urged his countrymen to donate generously to the Taliban:** Robert Lacey, *Inside the Kingdom: Kings, Clerics, Modernists, Terrorists and the Struggle for Saudi Arabia*, Penguin Group: London, 2009, 198.

68 **Secretary of State Hillary Clinton clearly understood where the money trail began:** "US Embassy Cables: Hillary Clinton

says Saudi Arabia 'a critical source of terrorist funding'" *The Guardian*, December 5, 2010, https://www.theguardian.com /world/us-embassy-cables-documents/242073.

Decklan Walsh, "WikiLeaks cables portray Saudi Arabia as a cash machine for terrorists," *The Guardian*, December 10, 2010.

69 **European Parliament:** Karen Armstrong, "Wahhabism to ISIS: How Saudi Arabia exported the main source of global terrorism," *The New Statesman*, November 27, 2014, https:// www.newstatesman.com/world-affairs/2014/11/ikipedia-isis -how-saudi-arabia-exported-main-source-global-terrorism.

69 **The Saudis have exported more extreme ideology:** Rudy Takala, "Hacked: Clinton said Saudis responsible for exporting 'extreme ideology,'" *Washington Examiner* October 9, 2016, https://www.washingtonexaminer.com/hacked-clinton-said -saudis-responsible-for-exporting-extreme-ideology.

70 **Riyadh has invested more than ten billion dollars:** Telegraph Reporters, "What is Wahhabism? The reactionary branch of Islam from Saudi Arabia said to be 'the main source of global terrorism,'" *The Daily Telegraph*, May 19, 2017. https:// www.telegraph.co.uk/news/2016/03/29/what-is-wahhabism -the-reactionary-branch-of-islam-said-to-be-the/.

70 **European Union intelligence:** Paul Vallely and Peter Waldman, "How Islamic State has forced its many enemies to work together," *The World*, August 28, 2014. https://www.theworldweekly.com /reader/view/292/how-islamic-state-has-forced-its-many-enemies -to-work-together.

CHAPTER 6

74 **Some xenophobic Saudis called it the "great betrayal":** Max Fisher, "9 Questions about Saudi Arabia you were too embarrassed to ask," *VOX*, January 26, 2015, https://www.vox.com /2015/1/26/7877619/saudi-arabia-questions.

74 **The final Senate report on 9/11:** David Smith, "9/11 report's classified '28 pages' about potential Saudi Arabia ties released," *The Guardian*, July 15, 2016, https://www.theguardian.com /us-news/2016/jul/15/911-report-saudi-arabia-28-pages -released.

Deb Riechmann, "After 13-year wait, 28 secret pages of 9/11 inquiry released," *PBS News Hour*, July 15, 2016, https://www.pbs.org/newshour/nation/13-year-wait-28 -pages-911-inquiry-will-released.

75 **Ba'athists:** The Arab Socialist Ba'ath Party is a political party founded in 1951 by Fuad al-Rikabi. De-Ba'athification refers to a policy undertaken in Iraq by the Coalition Provisional Authority (CPA) and subsequent Iraqi governments to remove the Ba'ath Party's influence in the new Iraqi political system.

Paul Bremer, "Coalition Provisional Authority Order Number 1: De-Ba'athification of Iraqi Society," May 16, 2003.

76 **Abu Ghraib and Camp Bucca:** Michael Weiss and Hassan Hassan, "ISIS used a US Prison as Boot Camp," *Daily Beast*, Feb 23, 2015, https://www.thedailybeast.com/isis-used-a-us -prison-as-boot-camp.

78 **Abu Bakr al-Baghdadi:** Full name Ibrahim Awad Ibrahim al-Badri, he is the leader of ISIS/ISIL/DAESH. Hannah Strange, "Islamic State leader Abu Bakr al-Baghdadi addresses Muslims in Mosul," *The Daily Telegraph*, July 5, 2014, https:// www.telegraph.co.uk/news/worldnews/middleeast/iki/10948480 /Islamic-State-leader-Abu-Bakr-al-Baghdadi-addresses-Muslims -in-Mosul.html.

79 **Vice President Joe Biden giving a lecture at Harvard's Kennedy School:** On Thursday, October 2, 2014, the 47th Vice President of the United States delivered a public address on foreign policy to the JFK Jr. Forum. Joe Biden, Lecture at Harvard University, Kennedy School of Government, Institute of Politics. October 2, 2014, https://www.youtube.com /watch?v=25aDP7io30U.

79 **A recently leaked confidential email:** Ben Norton, "Leaked Hillary Clinton emails show U.S. allies Saudi Arabia and Qatar supported ISIS," *Salon*, October 11, 2016. https://www.salon .com/2016/10/11/leaked-hillary-clinton-emails-show-u-s-allie s-saudi-arabia-and-qatar-supported-isis/.

CHAPTER 8

95 *Parabola:* "Learning on the Moment: A Conversation with Peter Brook," *Parabola: Sacred Dance*, 4:2,1979.

96 **Ayatollah Khomeini spoke out:** Samir Rahim, "Two books about revolutionary Iran by James Buchan and Michael Axworthy: Review," *The Daily Telegraph*, March 4, 2013.

99 **"Every day is Ashura, every land is Karbala":** Shahram Khosravi, *Young and Defiant in Tehran*, University of Pennsylvania Press: Philadelphia, 2008, 51.

100 **"I drink the chalice of poison":** Michael Axworthy, *Revolutionary Iran: A History of the Islamic Republic*, Oxford University Press: New York, 2013, 281.

CHAPTER 9

102 **Huston Smith:** Born in China in 1919, Huston Smith studied at Central Methodist University and the University of Chicago in the United States. He taught at the University of Denver, Washington University, MIT, and Syracuse University, where he was Thomas J. Watson Professor of Religion and Distinguished Adjunct Professor of Philosophy. His book, *The World's Religions*, sold over three million copies. James Fadiman and Robert Frager, *The Essential Sufism*, Harper-Collins: San Francisco, 1997, ix.

102 **Ibn Arabi describes:** Abu Bakr ibn al-Arabi, born in Sevilla in 1076 and died in Fez in 1148, was a judge and scholar of

Maliki law from al-Andalus. Ibn Arabi is cited in the website of the Golden Sufi Center that principally follows the Naqshbandi school. https://goldensufi.org/book_toc_chap_lovefire .html.

103 **fourteenth-century poet Hafez:** Khwāja Shams-ud-Dīn Muḥammad Ḥāfeẓ-e Shīrāzī (b: 1315, d: 1390) was a Persian poet, known by his penname Hafez, who wrote about love, faith, and exposing hypocrisy. His poem, "I Have Learned So Much," can be found in Daniel Ladinsky's *The Gift*.

104 **Federico García Lorca:** Federico del Sagrado Corazón de Jesús García Lorca (b: 6/5/1898, d: 8/18/1936), was a Spanish poet, playwright, and theater director. The quote about Hafez can be found in *Deep Song*, a lecture he gave in Granada on February 19, 1922. https://www.poetryintranslation.com/PITBR /Spanish/DeepSong.php.

104 **"Hafez has no peer":** Daniel Ladinsky, "The Mystical Poet that can help you lead a better Life" BBC, January 9, 2017, http://www.bbc.com/culture/story/20170109-the-mystical-poet -who-can-help-you-lead-a-better-life.

104 **"The Persian Lesson":** "The Persian Lesson" was originally titled "The Sufi Lesson." The Walt Whitman Archive, https:// whitmanarchive.org/published/LG/1891/poems/390.

105 ***What is the meaning:*** Elizabeth Gray, *The Green Sea of Heaven: Fifty Ghazals from the Diwan of Hafiz*, White Cloud Press: Ashland, 1995.

105 *Do not judge us:* Elizabeth Gray, *The Green Sea of Heaven: Fifty Ghazals from the Diwan of Hafiz*, White Cloud Press: Ashland, 1995.

106 **Even Queen Victoria:** Daniel Ladinsky, "The Mystical Poet that can help you lead a better Life" BBC, January 9, 2017, http://www.bbc.com/culture/story/20170109-the-mystical-poet -who-can-help-you-lead-a-better-life.

107 **Saadi Shirazi:** Saadi Shirazi lived from 1210 to 1292. Born in Shiraz, his most famed collection of poetry was entitled *Gulistan.* He traveled widely throughout the Middle East, India and part of China and saw many wars, devastations and inhumanities during the Mongol invasions which prompted him to write this poem, "Children of Adam." https://en.wikipedia .org/wiki/Saadi_Shirazi.

CHAPTER 10

114 **ten public relations firms:** Megan Wilson, "Saudi Arabia hires 10th Lobby firm," *The Hill*, October 3, 2016, http:// thehill.com/business-a-lobbying/lobbying-hires/298975 -saudi-arabia-hires-tenth-lobby-firm.

114 **"dangerous deformations":** Robert Fisk, "For the first time, Saudi Arabia is being attacked by both Sunni and Shia leaders," *The Independent*, September 22, 2016, https://www .independent.co.uk/voices/saudi-arabia-attacked-sunni-shia -leaders-wahhabism-chechenya-robert-fisk-a7322716.html.

115 **"If the world is looking forward to uprooting terrorism,":** Dr. Adil Rashid, "Et tu, Brute? After Shia Iran, the Sunni stab at Wahhabism," *WION*, October 14, 2016, http://www .wionews.com/world/et-tu-brute-after-shia-iran-the-sunni-stab -at-wahhabism-7448.

115 **"The Chechen Conference should serve as a wake-up":** Two articles on the site Al-Monitor cited the conference, but now they are no longer on the server, which raises a question about their dis- appearance. http://www.al-monitor.com/pulse/originals/2016/09 /egypt-saudi-arabia-controversy-grozny-conference-azhar.html http://www.al-monitor.com/pulse/originals/2016/09/iran-saudi -war-of-words-grand-mufti-khamenei.html.

115 **Muhammad al-Shaikh tweeted:** Sharmine Narwani, "From religion to politics, Saudi Arabia feeling chill of isolation," *Russia Today*, September 15, 2016, https://www.rt.com/op-ed /359409-religion-politics-saudi-isolation/.

116 **"We have to understand":** Al Waght, "Differences between Saudi Arabia, Egypt," *The Iran Project*, September 30, 2016, https://theiranproject.com/blog/2016/09/30/differences-saudi -arabia-egypt/

CHAPTER 11

122 **four L's:** Tariq Ramadan, "Muslims Need to Reform Their Minds," *The Guardian*, February 28, 2017, https://www. theguardian.com/world/2017/feb/28/tariq-ramadan-muslims -need-to-reform-their-minds.

CHAPTER 12

127 **He enjoyed great popularity:** Fuska Evani, "Ahok defies critics: increases popularity: political expert," *The Jakarta Globe* June 23, 2016, http://jakartaglobe.id/news/ahok-defies -critics-increases-popularity-political-expert/.

129 **150 mosques across Indonesia as well as one hundred *pesantrens*:** Margaret Scott, "Indonesia: The Saudis Are Coming," *New York Review of Books*, October 27, 2016, http://www .nybooks.com/articles/2016/10/27/indonesia-the-saudis-are -coming/.

131 **a 681 million-dollar gift:** Philip Sherwell, "Payment of $681m into accounts of Malaysian PM 'was a gift from Saudi royals,'" *Daily Telegraph*, January 26, 2016, https://www.telegraph. co.uknews/worldnews/asia/malaysia/12121546/Payment-of -681m-into-accounts-of-Malaysian-PM-was-a-gift-from-Saudi -royals.html.

131 **Asri Zainul Abidin:** Associate Professor Dato' Dr. Mohd Asri Zainul Abidin (b: 1/1/1971) is a popular independent Islamic preacher, writer, lecturer, and Islamic consultant from Malaysia. His quote about the banning of Shiites can be found in the *Boston Globe* article "In otherwise tolerant Malaysia, Shiites are banned." http://archive.boston.com/news/world/asia/articles/2011/01/14 /in_otherwise_tolerant_malaysia_shiites_are_banned/.

132 **Asghar Farhadi, boycotted the Academy Awards:** Alex Stedman, "Iranian Director Blasts 'Inhumane' Travel Ban in Statement After Winning Oscar," *Variety*, February 26, 2017,

http://variety.com/2017/film/news/asghar-farhadi-oscars-2017
-trump-travel-ban-1201997203/.

132 **Trump spoke strongly against terrorism:** Fareed Zakaria,
"How Saudi Arabia Played Donald Trump," *Washington Post,*
May 25, 2017, https://www.washingtonpost.com/opinions/
global-opinions/saudi-arabia-just-played-donald-trump/2017
/05/25/d0932702-4184-11e7-8c25-44d09ff5a4a8_story.html
?utm_term=.f820d8b6b567.

133 **Charles Glass, reporting on the event:** Charles Glass, "Card
trick at the House of Saud: Why Trump's Saudi Arabia claim
makes little sense to Christians and Muslims," *The Tablet,*
June 28, 2017, http://www.thetablet.co.uk/featurdes/2/10358
/card-trick-at-the-house-of-saud-why-trump-s-saudi-arabia
-claim-makes-little-sense-to-christians-and-muslims.

134 **King Abdullah of Jordan spoke:** "King attends Arab Islamic
American summit in Saudi Arabia," *The Jordan Times,* May
21, 2017, http://www.jordantimes.com/news/local/king-attends
-arab-islamic-american-summit-saudi-arabia.

137 **Theresa May, made a shocking announcement and suppressed the report:** Adam Bienkov, "Theresa May buries
international terror funding report for 'national security reasons'"
Business Insider UK, July 12, 2017, http://uk.businessinsider
.com/theresa-may-buries-international-terror-funding-report
-for-national-security-reasons-2017-7?IR=T.

CHAPTER 13

140 **He got a quick rebuke from Thomas Erdbrink:** https://
twitter.com/thomaserdbrink/status/934008818903678976
?lang=en.

141 **the Saudi government had spent eighteen million dollars:** Bethany Allen-Ebrahimian, "Qatar's Ramped-Up Lobbying Efforts Find Success in Washington," *Foreign Policy*,
February 6, 2018, http://foreignpolicy.com/2018/02/06/qatars
-ramped-up-lobbying-efforts-find-success-in-washington/.

141 **This act was then followed by a sweeping crescendo of
anti-corruption arrests:** Lyse Doucet, "Riyadh's night of
long knives and long-range missiles," BBC, November 6, 2017,
http://www.bbc.com/news/world-middle-east-41893694.

142 **France 24 flashed the headline:** "Saudi Arabia's anti-
corruption prince buys $300 million French chateau," *News
wires*, France 24, December 17, 2017, http://www.france24
.com/en/20171217-saudi-crown-prince-mohammed-salman
-buys-300-million-french-chateau.

143 **Doha stood accused of financing terrorism:** Tamara Qiblawi,
"Qatar rift: Saudi, UAE, Bahrain, Egypt cut diplomatic ties,"
CNN, July 27, 2017, https://edition.cnn.com/2017/06/05
/middleeast/saudi-bahrain-egypt-uae-qatar-terror/index.html.

143 **The Saudi military campaign estimated to have cost $100
billion:** Yoel Guzansky, "Saudi Arabia's War in Yemen Has
Been a Disaster," *The National Interest*, March 25, 2018,

http://nationalinterest.org/feature/saudi-arabias-war-yemen
-has-been-disaster-25064.

143 **The UN called it "the world's worst humanitarian crisis":**
"UN Agencies: Yemen Humanitarian Crisis Worst in World,"
VOA News, December 30, 2017, https://www.voanews.com/a
/un-agencies-yemen-humanitarian-crisis/4185462.html.

144 **One recent report by** *Conflict Armament Research***:**
Choi, David, "ISIS may have obtained anti-tank missiles from
the CIA," *Business Insider*, December 15, 2017, http://www
.businessinsider.com/isis-weapons-cia-missile-anti-tank-2017
-12?IR=T.

Brian Castner, "Exclusive: Tracing ISIS' weapons supply
chain—Back to the US," *Wired*, December 12, 2017,
https://www.wired.com/story/terror-industrial-complex
-isis-munitions-supply-chain/.

Tom O'Connor, "How ISIS Got Weapons from The U.S.
and Used Them To Take Iraq and Syria," *Newsweek*,
December 14, 2017, http://www.newsweek.com/how-isis
-got-weapons-us-used-them-take-iraq-syria-748468.

146 **"The Golden Road to Samarkand":** James Elroy Flecker,
The collected poems of James Elroy Flecker, 1884–1915. New
York: Doubleday, Page & Co., 1916.

147 **Ulugh Beg inspired not only Galileo but generations of
star gazers thereafter:** While Galileo did not know of Beg's

work directly, Beg contributed to the synchronicity of research
that would help Galileo with his own discoveries.

148 **Naqshband today is one of the largest Sufi orders in the
world with millions of followers:** Svante Cornell, "The
Naqshbandi-Khalidi Order and Political Islam in Turkey,"
The Hudson Institute, September 3, 2015, https://www
.hudson.org/research/11601-the-naqshbandi-khalidi-order-and
-political-islam-in-turkey.

SELECTED BIBLIOGRAPHY

Aarts, Paul and Carolien Roelants. *Saudi Arabia: A Kingdom in Peril.* Cambridge University Press: Cambridge, 2015.

Al-Rasheed, Madawi. *Contesting the Saudi State: Islamic Voices from a New Generation.* Cambridge University Press: Cambridge, 2006.

Arberry, A.J. *The Koran Interpreted.* George Allen & Unwin Ltd: London, 1935.

Axworthy, Michael, *Revolutionary Iran: A History of the Islamic Republic.* Oxford University Press: New York, 2013.

Borges, Jorge Luis. *Seven Nights.* New Directions Publishing: New York, 1984.

Bradley, John. *Saudi Arabia Exposed: Inside a Kingdom in Crisis.* St. Martin's Press: New York, 2015.

Bunzel, Cole. *From Paper State to Caliphate: The Ideology of the Islamic State.* Center for Middle East Policy, The Brookings Institution: Washington D.C., 2015.

Bunzel, Cole. *The Kingdom and the Caliphate: Duel of the Islamic States.* Carnegie Endowment for Peace: New York, 2016.

Cockburn, Patrick. *Age of Jihad: Islamic State and the Great War for the Middle East.* Verso: New York, 2016.

Cockburn, Patrick. *The Rise of the Islamic State: ISIS and the New Sunni Revolution.* Random House: New York, 2015.

Cortas, Wadad Makdisi. *A World I Loved: The Story of an Arab Woman.* Nation Books: New York, 2009.

Commins, David. *Islam in Saudi Arabia.* Cornell University Press: Ithaca, 2015.

Fadiman, James and Robert Frager. *The Essential Sufism.* Harper-Collins: San Francisco, 1997.

Ghattas, Kim. *Black Wave: Saudi Arabia, Iran, and the Forty-Year Rivalry That Unraveled Culture, Religion and the Collective Memory in the Middle East.* Henry Holt: New York, NY, 2020.

Glass, Charles. *Syria Burning: The Rise of ISIS and the Death of the Arab Spring.* OR Books: London, 2015.

Gray, Elizabeth. *The Green Sea of Heaven: Fifty Ghazals from the Diwan of Hafiz.* White Cloud Press, 1995.

Hafez, and Dick Davies. *Faces of Love: Hafez and the Poets of Shiraz.* Penguin Classics: London, 2013.

Hafiz, and Daniel Landinsky. *The Gift: Poems by Hafiz, the Great Sufi Master.* Compass: New York, 2009.

Hafiz, *The Garden of Heaven: Poems of Hafiz,* Trans. Gertrude Bell, Dover Editions: London, 2003.

Hegghammer, Thomas. *Jihad in Saudi Arabia: Violence and Pan-Islamism Since 1979.* Cambridge University Press: Cambridge, 2010.

Hubbard, Ben. *MBS: The Rise to Power of Mohammed bin Salman.* Tim Duggan Books: New York, NY, 2020.

Khosravi, Shahram. *Young and Defiant in Tehran.* University of Pennsylvania Press: Philadelphia, 2008.

Lacey, Robert. *Inside the Kingdom: Kings, Clerics, Modernists, Terrorists and the Struggle for Saudi Arabia*. Penguin Group: London, 2009.

Lippman, Thomas. *Saudi Arabia on the Edge*. Potomac Books (Council on Foreign Relations): New York, 2012.

Maalouf, Amin. *The Crusades Through Arab Eyes*. Saqi Books: London, 1984.

Maalouf, Amin. *Samarkand*. Hachette: London, 1994.

Matthiesen, Toby. *The Other Saudis: Shiism, Dissent and Sectarianism*. Cambridge University Press: Cambridge, 2014.

Menoret, Pascal. *Graveyard of Clerics: Everyday Activism in Saudi Arabia*. Stanford University Press: Palo Alto, 2020.

Mottahedeh, Roy. *The Mantle of the Prophet: Religion and Politics in Iran*. Pantheon Books: New York, 1985.

Nasr, Seyyed Hossein, Carner Dagli, and Fioretta Dakake. *The Study Quran: A New Translation and Commentary*. HarperCollins: New York, 2015.

Nasr, Vali. *The Shia Revival*. W. W. Norton & Company: New York, 2007.

Rumi, Jalaladdin and Coleman Barks. *The Essential Rumi*. HarperCollins: New York, 2010.

Ramadan, Tariq. *Islam: The Essentials*. Penguin Books: New York, 2017.

Sadar, Ziauddin. *Mecca: The Sacred City*. Bloomsbury USA: New York, 2014.

Said, Edward. *Covering Islam: How the Media and the Experts Determine How We See the Rest of the World*. Vintage Books: New York, 1979.

Said, Edward. *Orientalism*. Vintage Books: New York, 1979.

Schaht, Joseph. *The Legacy of Islam*. Oxford University Press: Oxford, 1979.

Tarsin, Asad. *Being Muslim: A Practical Guide*. Sandala: Berkeley, 2015.

Valentine, Simon Ross. *Force and Fanaticism: Wahhabism in Saudi Arabia and Beyond*. Hurst Publishers: London, 2016.

Weiss, Michael and Hassan Hassan. *ISIS: Inside the Army of Terror*. Regan Arts: New York, 2015.

Zareef, Abdul Salam. *My Life with The Taliban*. Hurst Publishers: London, 2011.

ARTICLES

Al-Nabi. "al-Shaykh al-Baghdadi ala khuta l-imam Muhammad ibn Abd al-Wahhab: al-tashabuh bayn al-dawlatayn al-Wahhabiyya wal-Baghdadiyya" [Sheikh Baghdadi in the footsteps of Muhammad ibn Abd al-Wahhab: The resemblance between the Wahhabi and Baghdadi States]. *Muassasat al-Minhaj*, December 31, 2014.

Al-Sururiyya, Gharib. "Sirat aimmat al-Islam fi hadm mawadi al-shirk wal-tughyan" [The way of the imams of Islam in destroying places of unbelief and oppression]. *Muassasat al-Minhaj*, July 23, 2015.

Al-Juburi, Muharib. "al-Ilan an qiyam Dawlat al-Iraq al-Islamiyya" [The announcement of the Islamic State of Iraq]. October 15, 2006, in *al-Majmu liqadat Dawlat al-Iraq al-Islamiyya* [The anthology [of statements] of the leaders of the Islamic State of Iraq], Nukhbat al-Ilam al-Jihadi, 2010.

Al-Rashid, Madawi. "Is Saudi Arabia to blame for the Islamic State?" BBC, December 19, 2015.

Alfan, Rheza. "Political Indicators: Society Satisfied with Ahok Performance." *Tirto.id*, January 26, 2017.

Ali-Bhai Brown, Yasmine. "The Evil Empire of Saudi Arabia is the West's Real Enemy." *The Independent*, September 27, 2015.

Al Waght. "Differences between Saudi Arabia, Egypt." *Iran Project*, September 30, 2016.

Allen-Ebrahimian, Bethany. "Qatar's Ramped-Up Lobbying Efforts Find Success in Washington." *Foreign Policy*, February 6, 2018.

Apuzzo, Matt and Mark Mazzetti. "US Relies Heavily on Saudi Money to Support Syrian Rebels." *New York Times*, January 23, 2016. https://www.nytimes.com/2016/01/24/world/middleeast /us-relies-heavily-on-saudi-money-to-support-syrian-rebels.html.

Armstrong, Karen. "Wahhabism to ISIS: How Saudi Arabia exported the main source of global terrorism." *The New Statesman*, November 27, 2014.

Asthana, Anushka. "Theresa May accused of double standards over terrorism funding." *The Guardian*, July 6, 2017.

Bienkov, Adam. "Theresa May buries international terror funding report for 'national security reasons'" *Business Insider UK*, July 12, 2017.

Callamachi, Rukmini. "ISIS Enshrines a Theology of Rape." *New York Times*, August 13, 2015.

Callamachi, Rukmini. "To the World they are Muslims. To ISIS, Sufis are Heretics," *New York Times*, November 25, 2017.

Clemens, Steve. "Thank God for the Saudis, ISIS, Iraq, and the Lessons Blowback," *The Atlantic*, June 23, 2014.

Calamur, Krishnadev. "Nine Years for the Cultural Destruction of Timbuktoo," *The Atlantic*, September 27, 2016, p. 33.

Castner, Brian. "Exclusive: Tracing ISIS' weapons supply chain—Back to the US," *Wired*, December 12, 2017.

Choi, David. "ISIS may have obtained anti-tank missiles from the CIA." *Business Insider*, December 15, 2017.

Cockburn, Patrick. "How Obama Turned His Back on Saudi Arabia and Its Sunni Allies." *The Independent*, March 12, 2016.

Cockburn, Patrick. "Iraq Crisis: How Saudi Arabia helped Isis take over the north of the Country." *The Independent*, July 12, 2014.

Cockburn, Patrick. "This Spread of Holy Fascism is a Disaster." *The Independent*, May 17, 2014.

Cornell, Svante. "The Naqshbandi-Khalidi Order and Political Islam in Turkey." *The Hudson Institute*, September 3, 2015.

Creidi, Imam. "In demanding Hariri's return, Lebanese find rare unity." *Reuters* November 12, 2017.

Daoud, Kamal. "Saudi Arabia, an ISIS That Has Made It." *New York Times*, November 20, 2015. https://www.nytimes.com/2015/11/21/opinion/saudi-arabia-an-isis-that-has-made-it.html.

Digest Middle East. "How Islamic State has forced its many enemies to work together." *The World*, August 28, 2014.

Doucet, Lyse. "Riyadh's night of long knives and long-range missiles." *BBC*, November 6, 2017.

Editorial Board. "Fighting while Funding Extremists." *New York Times*, June 19, 2017.

Elgot, Jessica. "Theresa May sitting on report on foreign funding of UK extremists." *The Guardian*, July 3, 2017.

Evani, Fuska. "Ahok defies critics: increases popularity: political expert." *The Jakarta Globe*, June 23, 2016.

Fisher, Max. "9 Questions about Saudi Arabia you were too embarrassed to ask." *VOX*, January 26, 2015.

Fisk, Robert. "For the first time, Saudi Arabia is being attacked by both Sunni and Shia leaders." *The Independent*, September 22, 2016.

Fisk, Robert. "Saudi Arabia: the history of hypocrisy that we chose to ignore." *The Independent*, January 14, 2015.

Friedman, Tom. "Saudi Arabia's Arab Spring at Last." *New York Times*. November 23, 2017.

Ghosh, Bobby. "How Mohammad Bin Salman Hit a Dead End in Washington." Bloomberg. May 4, 2020. https://www.bloombergquint.com/gadfly/saudi-arabia-s-crown-prince-mbs-is-right-where-trump-wants-him.

Glass, Charles. "Card trick at the House of Saud: Why Trump's Saudi Arabia claim makes little sense to Christians and Muslims." *The Tablet*, June 28, 2017.

Guzansky, Yoel. "Saudi Arabia's War in Yemen Has Been a Disaster." *The National Interest*, March 25, 2018.

Haykel, Bernard. "Is Saudi Arabia to blame for the Islamic State?" *BBC*, 19 December 2015.

Haykel, Bernard. "On the Nature of Salafi Thought and Action." *Global Salafism: Islam's New Religious Movement*. Ed. Roel Meijer. Hurst, London 2009.

Howden, Daniel. "The Destruction of Mecca: Saudi hardliners are wiping out their own heritage." *The Independent*, August 5, 2005.

Hubbard, Ben. "ISIS Turns Saudis against the Kingdom, and Families Against Their Own." *New York Times,* March 31, 2016. https://www.nytimes.com/2016/04/01/world/middleeast/isis-saudi-arabia-wahhabism.html.

Hubbard, Ben. "Saudis Turn Birthplace of Wahhabism Ideology into a Tourist Spot." *New York Times,* May 31, 2015. https://www.nytimes.com/2015/06/01/world/middleeast/saudis-turn-birthplace-of-ideology-into-tourist-spot.html.

Hubbard, Ben. "Secrets of the Kingdom: A Fundamentalist Creed." *New York Times,* May 31, 2016.

Jalabi, Raya. "After the Hajj: Mecca Residents Grow Hostile to Changes in the Holy City." *The Guardian,* September 14, 2016.

Jenkins, Ron. "THEATER; An Iranian Musical Spectacle That Draws Audiences." New York Times, July 7, 2002.

Jeremy Bob, Jonah. "It's A New World—Where Israel Shares Intelligence With The Saudis." *Jerusalem Post,* November 19, 2017.

JT. "King attends Arab Islamic American summit in Saudi Arabia." *The Jordan Times,* May 21, 2017.

Kerr, Simon. "Saudi Arabia to launch global PR offensive to counter negative press." *Financial Times,* September 12, 2017.

Kinzer, Stephen. "Saudi Arabia is De-stabilizing the World." *Boston Globe,* June 7, 2016.

Kirkpatrick, David. "ISIS' Harsh Brand of Islam Is Rooted in Austere Saudi Creed." *New York Times,* September 24, 2014.

Ladinsky, Daniel. "The Mystical Poet that can help you lead a better Life." *BBC,* January 9, 2017.

Lazare, Daniel. "How U.S.–Saudi Marriage Gave Birth to Jihad" *The American Conservative,* November 2, 2017.

Morgan, David. "Wikileaks: Saudis Largest Source of World Terror." *CBS News*, December 5, 2010.

McDowall, Angus, "Inside the Saudi Prison That's Home to New Wave of Jihadis," *Reuters*, July 6, 2015.

Narwani, Sharmine. "From religion to politics, Saudi Arabia feeling chill of isolation." *Russia Today*, September 15, 2016.

Nehme, Dalia. "Saudi Arabia and Iran in war of words before the hajj, where hundreds were trampled last year." *Business Insider*, September 7, 2016.

Ng, Eileen. "In otherwise tolerant Malaysia, Shiites are banned." *Boston Globe*, January 14, 2011.

Norton, Ben. "Leaked Hillary Clinton emails show U.S. allies Saudi Arabia and Qatar supported ISIS." *Salon*, October 11, 2016.

O'Connor, Tom. "How ISIS Got Weapons from The U.S. And Used Them To Take Iraq And Syria." *Newsweek*, December 14, 2017.

Pfeiffer, Alex. "New York Times Friedman Slammed for puff piece on Saudi Royal." *The Daily Caller*, November 24, 2017.

Qiblawi, Tamara. "Qatar rift: Saudi, UAE, Bahrain, Egypt cut diplomatic ties." *CNN*, July 27, 2017.

Rahim, Samir. "Two books about revolutionary Iran by James Buchan and Michael Axworthy: Review." *The Daily Telegraph*, March 4, 2013, 69.

Ramadan, Tariq. "Muslims Need to Reform Their Minds." *The Guardian*, February 28, 2017.

Rasheed, Dr. Adil. "Et tu, Brute? After Shia Iran, the Sunni stab at Wahhabism." *WION*, October 14, 2016.

Riechmann, Deb. "After 13-year wait, 28 secret pages of 9/11 inquiry released." PBS, July 15, 2016.

Sanger, David. "US in a Bind as Saudi Actions Test a Durable Alliance." *New York Times*, January 4, 2016. https://www.nytimes.com/2016/01/05/us/politics/us-struggles-to-explain-alliance-with-saudis.html.

Sardar, Ziauddin. "The Destruction of Mecca." *New York Times*, September 30, 2014.

"Saudi Arabia's anti-corruption prince buys $300 million French chateau." News wires, *France 24*, December 17, 2017.

"Saudi Regime Hell-bent on Wiping Muslim Heritage in Hejaz." *Islam Times*. August 30, 2019. https://www.islamtimes.org/en/news/813551/saudi-regime-hell-bent-on-wiping-muslim-heritage-in-hejaz.

Scott, Margaret. "The Saudis are Coming." *New York Review of Books*, October 27, 2016.

Shane, Scott. "Saudis and Extremism: Both Arsonists and the Firefighters." *New York Times*, August 25, 2016.

Sherwell, Philip. "Payment of $681m into accounts of Malaysian PM 'was a gift from Saudi royals.'" *Daily Telegraph*, January 26, 2016.

Smith, David. "9/11 report's classified '28 pages' about potential Saudi Arabia ties released." *The Guardian*, July 15, 2016.

Steinberg, Guido. "The Wahhabiyya and Shi'ism, from 1744/45 to 2008." in *The Sunna and Shi'a in History: Division and Ecumenism in the Muslim Middle East* ed. Ofra Bengio and Meir Litvak. Palgrave, New York, 2011.

Steinhauser, Gabriele. "Islamist Sentenced to Nine Years for Timbuktu Shrine Destruction." *Wall Street Journal*, September 27, 2016.

Strange, Hannah. "Islamic State leader Abu Bakr al-Baghdadi addresses Muslims in Mosul." *The Daily Telegraph*, July 5, 2014.

Takala, Rudy, "Hacked: Clinton said Saudis responsible for exporting 'extreme ideology.'" *Washington Examiner*, October 9, 2016.

Taylor, Jerome, "Mecca for the Rich: Islam's holiest site being 'turning into Vegas'" *The Independent*, September 23, 2011.

Telegraph Reporters, "What is Wahhabism? The reactionary branch of Islam from Saudi Arabia said to be 'the main source of global terrorism.'" *The Daily Telegraph*, May 19, 2017.

US Dept of Treasury, Testimony of Stuart Levey, Under Secretary Office of Terrorism and Financial Intelligence U.S. Department of the Treasury Before the Senate Committee on Banking, Housing, and Urban Affairs, July 13, 2005.

"US Embassy Cables: Hillary Clinton says Saudi Arabia 'a critical source of terrorist funding.'" *The Guardian*, December 5, 2010.

Ward, Terence. "The Chilling Message of the Saudi Executions." CNN. May 9, 2019. https://edition.cnn.com/2019/05/08/opinions /saudi-arabia-shia-executions-message-ward/index.html.

Weiss, Michael and Hassan Hassan. "ISIS used a US Prison as Boot Camp." *Daily Beast*, Feb 23, 2015.

Wilson, Megan. "Saudi Arabia hires 10th Lobby firm." *The Hill*, October 3, 2016.

Wilson, Tom. "Does Qatar Support Extremism? Yes. And So Does Saudi Arabia." *New York Times*, August 10, 2017.

Zakaria, Fareed. "How Saudi Arabia Played Donald Trump." *Washington Post*, May 25, 2017.

Zakaria, Fareed. "Saudi Arabia, the Devil We Know." *Washington Post*, April 21, 2016.

VIDEOS

Alaoudh, Abdullah, "MBS is Not Saudi Arabia" Interview with Saudi scholar, Al-Jazeera TV, (June 28, 2019). https://www.aljazeera.com/programmes/talktojazeera/2019/06/saudi-scholar-alaoudh-mbs-saudi-arabia-190626131438417.html.

al-Rasheed, Madawi, "The Saudi Lie." Talk by Griffith University, Conservatorium Theatre, South Brisbane, Queensland, Australia, October 26 2019. https://www.youtube.com/watch?v=BoDsE5Uh08E.

Amanpour, Christiane, and Terence Ward, "Author on the Link between Wahhabism and Jihad," CNN interview, December 21, 2018. https://edition.cnn.com/videos/tv/2018/12/21/amanpour-terence-ward-the-wahhabi-code-how-the-saudis-spread-extremism-globally.cnn.

Biden, Joe, "Lecture at Harvard University, Kennedy School School of Government, Institute of Politics," October 2, 2014, https://www.youtube.com/watch?v=25aDP7io30U.

"Leading Saudi Cleric: Daesh ISIS have the Same Beliefs as we do." MBC DUBAI, January 22, 2016, https://www.youtube.com/watch?v=GWORE6OBfhc.

DOCUMENTARIES

"Saudi Arabia Uncovered." *Frontline*, PBS, March 29, 2016.

"Yemen under Siege." *Frontline*, PBS, May 3, 2016.

"The Secret History of ISIS." *Frontline*, PBS, May 17, 2016.

"Confronting ISIS." *Frontline*, PBS, October 11, 2016.

"Terror in Europe." *Frontline*, PBS, October 18, 2016.